CLARENCE DARROW:
Lessons for Today's Lawyer

**by
Douglas Trant**

©Douglas A. Trant, 2004

ISBN 0-9639191-1-3

Douglas A. Trant
Attorney at Law
900 S. Gay Street
Suite 1502
Knoxville, TN 37902
(865) 525–7980
(865) 525–7896–Fax

dtrant@bellsouth.net
http://www.lawyers.com/trant-criminallaw

Dedication

Darrow had Ruby

and I, Janis, without whom neither of us could have success and happiness.

Publications

Contributing Author, "Tennessee Death Penalty Defense Manual," Tennessee Association of Criminal Defense Lawyers

Author: "Trial Manual for the Defense of Habitual Criminal Cases in Tennessee," 1985

"Cross-Examination of Government Scientific Witnesses," The Champion, September-October, 1993

"The Design of Justice," Dicta, Volume 26, Issue 9, October 20, 2000 - awarded best article for 2000

"A Plea for Chivalry," Dicta Volume 27, Issue 3, March 21, 2001

"Crime in America," International Society of Barristers Quarterly, Volume 35, No. 4, October 2000

"Killer Cross-Examinations," The Pit Bull, 1996"

"Justice Kidnapped, 2000"

"Pretrial Release: Community Ties to the 21st Century," The Champion, September-October 2003

Contents

CHAPTER 1	Jury Selection	1
CHAPTER 2	Cross-Examining the Expert	23
CHAPTER 3	Cross-Examination by Preparation	53
CHAPTER 4	Closing Argument–Pleading for Life	73
CHAPTER 5	Closing Argument–Attacking the State's Psychiatrist	101
CHAPTER 6	Closing Argument/Beating the Murder Rap	107

Introduction

Clarence Darrow was one of the greatest trial lawyers not only of his time, but of all times. The lessons that we can learn from him are as applicable today as they were in the first part of the 20th Century. This book will let lawyers learn by his words and deeds in court. Supplemented by my thoughts and my selected transcripts in which I seek to apply the lessons I have learned from this great trial lawyer.

Darrow in jury selection at State of Tennessee v. John Thomas Scopes

CHAPTER 1

JURY SELECTION

Whether a jury is a good one or a bad one depends on the point of view. I have always been an attorney for the defense. I can think of nothing, not even war, that has brought so much misery to the human race as prisons. And all of it is so futile!

Clarence Darrow

Attorney for the Defense Revisited

Nearly 70 years ago Darrow wrote his thoughts on jury selection for *Esquire* magazine. What he wrote is almost timeless. One can easily detect from that article two character traits that made him so successful-he knew about people and cared to know more.

In the 70 years since Darrow wrote much has been said or written about jury selection. Some psychologists specialize in jury selection and they conduct surveys, polls and profiles. Lawyers take acting classes to learn how to better communicate with jurors. Some even write articles on how lawyers should dress.

Darrow knew, however, that good jury selection boils down to a perceptive lawyer's intuition. We can get to know prospective jurors only slightly. We have to go on how we feel about them. We guess sometimes right, sometimes wrong. The good defense lawyer usually guesses right. Each lawyer can excuse a limited number of prospective jurors and we try to get rid of the bad ones, hoping we guess right about the remainder. Again, we do not try to pick a jury that will deliver justice; we try to pick one that will become part of our team.

Darrow knew that most people charged with crimes are poor people. Poor people often commit crimes because of their poverty. They have no political clout. Because of their lack of power and money, they have a harder time winning- whether they are guilty or innocent!

Darrow did indeed champion the underdog. He had to look for jurors who would feel for the underdog. He wrote, "the most important point to learn is whether the perspective juror is humane." We still search for that juror today. Every question we ask potential jurors, every factor we weigh, is designed to try to determine if that juror can feel for this defendant.

What factors should be considered? What information should we seek? Darrow considered national origin. Unfortunately, most jurors have been in the melting pot long enough now that national origin is not much of a factor. If, however, a juror comes from a family of recent immigrants, one should look for national trait such as the Irish possessed-"emotional kindly and sympathetic."

Darrow placed great emphasis on religion, and well he should. Darrow warned against Presbyterians. The Presbyterian "believes in John Calvin and eternal punishment." That is a deadly combination. Presbyterians also have to use a crow bar to open their wallets: property is sacred. One who steals that property must be of Satan.

"If possible, the Baptist are more hopeless than the Presbyterians." Again, Darrow's advice holds true today. They believe one who has committed a crime is destined for damnation, and they are only too happy to help him on his way.

Darrow also distrusted Lutherans. Quite possibly a combination of Martin Luther and frigid weather makes them too serious. One should be careful of them.

Darrow liked Methodists better. They were "nearer to the soil." Most Methodists are urban today, but more as then, they do tend to be more compassionate and tolerant. Now, as then, a contest between a Methodist and a Baptist is no contest.

Darrow's favorites were Catholics, Jews, Unitarians, and agnostics. Catholics as a rule should be kept. They are, as a group, some of the most compassionate people around. Jews are historically oppressed and should be left on the jury unless they are merchants. Then their economic loyalties outweigh their heritage of compassion. Unitarians are by far the best jurors if you can get them. Unfortunately there just are not that many. Finally, unlike Darrow, I have never had anyone own up to being an agnostic. You can bet that if I ever do; I'll keep him. The prosecutor would probably get rid of the "heathen" in a hurry, however!

Darrow cautioned against prohibitionists. Those days are gone, but we still have the same kind of person. Now he is a member of the moral majority. These people should not even be allowed to get their seats warm in the jury box. They are petty, vindictive, narrow-minded people. They could not care about someone accused of a crime if God spoke to them directly to instruct them so. Beware similarly of right-to-lifers.

Beware also of members of the VFW and American Legion. They fought for their country and love everything about it except the Bill of Rights. Unfortunately, that love does not extend to individual citizens who have never had the chances to do as well as they have.

Hunters and members of the National Rifle Association are also anathema. People who can shoot a poor defenseless animal have no difficulty convicting someone accused of a criminal act. Don't let them lower their sights on a defendant!

"Never take a wealthy man on a jury." Wealthy people in 1936 and today, must think the poor deserve to be poor to rationalize their own privileged position.

In 1936 a new group was entering the jury box-women. Seventy years later we know what we have always known. Women as a group are more emotional and care for their fellow human beings more than men do. The nurturing instinct is present on juries where women will sometimes want to mother a defendant. Do beware, however, on women hell-bent on making it in a man's world by being tougher than any man. Those women, I am sad to say, have forgotten how to care.

Age is another important factor to consider. Elderly people as a group seem to be the most compassionate. They have seen it all and have become more tolerant. My personal favorite is little old ladies. I would take twelve old ladies on a jury any day without any other questions asked unless of course, the victim of the crime was a little old lady.

Beware of middle-aged men. They think they should run the world and protect everyone in it from the dreaded criminal element. You will not often get much compassion from them.

People under twenty-five are usually a big disappointment. These days instead of being idealistic they worry more about how much property they can accumulate in the shortest amount of time. As a group, they show little concern for fellow humans.

Occupation should also be examined. Many professionals enjoy automatic excuses from jury duty. One certainly could make the argument that everyone should serve. Unfortunately that group includes nurturing professions such as nursing and teaching. Look for people who help others in their jobs; watch out for entrepreneurs. People interested only in making a buck are sure to vote guilty.

Intangibles must also be weighed. How does the juror react? Does he seem stiff, reserved, authoritarian? Or is he open, congenial, interested? How does he dress, sit, wear his hair? What books does he read, shows does he watch? Is he married? Does he call himself a liberal, conservative or moderate? Is he a Republican, Democrat or Independent? Give me the open, interested, liberal Democrat. Usher out the stiff, authoritarian, conservative Republican,

Look also at how the group of twelve gels. Who will be the leaders and who the followers? Who will go with the flow and who will ask the hard questions? Who, like Henry Fonda in *Twelve Angry Men,* will hold out for acquittal against tremendous pressure and who will give in too easily? Who will like you, the lawyer, enough to want to help you out?

Darrow did not have the pleasure of being able to select many blacks for his juries. Blacks better than any other group in our country understand crime, poverty and oppression. Black people know how hard it is to get a fair shake in our judicial system. They have not forgotten how to feel. Only in rare circumstances should a black be excused.

"You may defy all the rest of the rules if you can get a man who laughs. Few things in this world are of enough importance to warrant considering them seriously. So, by all means, choose a man who laughs. A juror who laughs hates to find anyone guilty."

Those words never rang truer. No factor is more important than a person's ability to be emotional. People who cannot laugh cannot feel. People who cannot feel surely will convict.

The overriding description of the criminal justice system for Darrow was "futile." The Courts will never solve crime. Crime is a social problem with many roots and the Courts are designed only to process crime. The law is sterile; the Courts are assembly lines-processing people into the penitentiary. Only by injecting people into the system who care-be they judges, lawyers or jurors-can any justice ever be done. Clarence Darrow was such a person. The by-word of the system will always be futility, but we must continue to care. We must continue to win.

ATTORNEY FOR THE DEFENSE
BY CLARENCE DARROW

The audience that storms the box-office of the theater to gain entrance to a sensational show is small and sleepy compared with the throng that crashes to the courthouse door when something concerning real life and death is to be laid bare to the public.

Everyone knows that the best portrayals of life are tame and sickly when matched with the realities. For this reason, the sophisticated Romans were wont to gather at the Colosseum to feast their eyes on fountains of real blood and await breathlessly the final thrust. The courtroom is a modern arena in which the greatest thrills follow closely on each other. If the combat concerns human life, it presents an atmosphere and setting not unlike those cruel and bloody scenes of ancient Rome. The judge wears the same flowing robe with all the dignity and superiority he can command. This sets him apart from his fellow-men, and is designed to awe and intimidate and to impress the audience with seeming wisdom oftener than with kindliness and compassion.

One cannot help wondering what happens to the pomp and pretense of the wearer while the cloak is in the wash, or while changing into a mature more monarchial mantle, as his bench becomes a throne, or when he strolls along the street in file with the "plain clothes" people.

When court opens, the bailiff intones some voodoo singsong words in an ominous voice that carries fear and respect at the opening of the rite. The courtroom is full of staring men and women shut within closed doors, guarded by officials wearing uniforms to confound the simple inside the sacred precinct. This dispels all hope of mercy to the unlettered, the poor and helpless, who scarcely dare express themselves above a whisper in any such forbidding place.

The stage, the arena, the court are alike in that each has its audience thirsting to drink deeply of the passing show. Those playing the parts vie for success and use whatever skill and talent they posses. An actor may fumble his lines, but a lawyer needs to be letter-perfect; at least, he has to use his wits, and he may forget himself, and often does, but never for a moment can he lose sight of his client.

Small wonder that ambitious, imaginative youths crowd the profession of law. Here, they feel, they themselves will find the opportunity to play a real part in the comedies as well as the tragedies of life. Everyone, no matter how small his chance may be, tries to hold the center of some stage where the multitudes will scan his every move. To most lads it seems as though the courts were organized to furnish them a chance to bask in the public eye. In this field the adventure of life will never pall, but prove interesting, exciting and changeful to the end. Not only will he have the destinies of men to protect and preserve, but his own standing and success to create.

If it is a real case, criminal or civil, it usually is tried by a jury with the assistance and direction of the judge. In that event, every moment counts, and neither the lawyers nor the audience, or even the court, goes to sleep. If it is a criminal case, or even a civil one, it is not the law alone or the facts that determine the results. Always the element of luck and chance looms large. A jury of twelve men is watching not only the evidence but the attitude of each lawyer, and the parties involved, in all their moves, Every step is fraught with doubt, if not mystery.

Selecting a jury is of the utmost importance. So far as possible, the lawyer should know both sides of the case. If the client is a landlord, a banker, or a manufacturer, or one of that type, then jurors sympathetic to that class will be wanted in the box; a man who looks neat and trim and smug. He will be sure to guard your interests as he would his own. His entire environment has taught him that all real values are measured in cash, and he knows no other worth. Every knowing lawyer seeks for a jury of the same sort of men as his client; men who will be able to imagine themselves in the same situation and realize what verdict the client wants.

Lawyers are just as carefully concerned about the likes and dislikes, the opinions and fads of judge as of jurors. All property rights are much safer in the hands of courts than of jurors. Every lawyer who represents the poor avoids a trial by the court.

Choosing jurors is always a delicate task. The more a lawyer knows of life, human nature, psychology, and the reactions of the human emotions, the better he is equipped for the subtle selection of his so-called "twelve men, good and true." In this undertaking, everything pertaining to the prospective juror needs to be questioned and weighed: his nationality, his business, religion, politics, social standing, family ties, friends, habits of life and thought; the books and newspapers he likes and reads, and many more matters that combine to make a man; all of these qualities and experiences have left their effect on ideas, beliefs and fancies that inhabit his mind. Understanding of all this cannot be obtained too bluntly. It usually requires finesse, subtlety and guesswork. Involved in it all is the juror's method of speech, the kind of clothes he wears, the style of haircut, and above all, his business associates, residence and origin.

To the ordinary observer, a man is just a man. To the student of life and human beings, every pose and movement is a part of the personality and the man. There is no sure rule by which one can gauge any person. A man may seem to be of a certain mold, but a wife, a friend, or an enemy, entering into his life, may change his most vital views, desires, and attitudes, so that he will hardly recognize himself as the man he once seemed to be.

It is obvious that if a litigant discovered one of his dearest friends in the jury panel he could make a close guess as to how certain facts, surrounding circumstances, and suppositions would affect his mind and action; but as he has no such acquaintance with the stranger before him, he must weigh the prospective juror's words and manner of speech and, in fact, hastily and cautiously "size him up" as best he can. The litigants and their lawyers are supposed to want justice, but in reality there is no such thing as justice, either in or out of court. In fact, the word cannot be defined. So, for lack of proof, let us assume that the word "justice" has a meaning, and that the common idea of the definition is correct, without even seeking to find out what is the common meaning. Then how do we reach justice through the courts? The lawyer's idea of justice is a verdict for his client, and really this is the sole end for which he aims.

In spite of the power that the courts exercise over the verdict of the jury, still the finding of the twelve men is very important, sometimes conclusive. It goes without saying that lawyers always do their utmost to get men on the jury who are apt to decide in favor of their clients. It is not the experience of jurors, neither is it their brain power that is the potent influence in their decisions. A skillful lawyer does not tire himself hunting for learning or intelligence in the box; if he knows much about man and his making, he knows that all beings act from emotions and instincts, and that reason is not a motive factor. If deliberation counts for anything, it is to retard decision. The nature of the man himself is the element that determines the juror's bias for or against his fellow-man. Assuming that a juror is not a half-wit, his intellect can always furnish fairly good reasons for following his instincts and emotions. Many irrelevant issues in choosing jurors are not so silly as they seem. Matters that apparently have nothing to do with the discussion of a case often are the greatest significance.

In the last analysis, most jury trials are contests between the rich and poor. If the case concerns money, it is apt to be a case of damages for injuries of some sort claimed to have been inflicted by someone. These cases are usually defended by insurance companies, railroads, or factories. If a criminal case, it is practically always the poor who are on trial.

The most important point to learn is whether the prospective juror is humane. This must be discovered in more or less devious ways. As soon as "the court" sees what you want, he almost always blocks the game. Next to this, in having more or less bearing on the questions, is the nationality, politics, and religion of the person examined for the jury. If you do not discover this, all your plans may go awry. Whether you are handling a damage suit, or your client is charged with the violation of law, his attorney will try to get the same sort of juror.

Let us assume that we represent one of "the underdogs" because of injuries received, or because of an indictment brought by what the prosecutors name themselves, "the state." Then what sort of men will we seek? An Irishman is called into the box for examination. There is no reason for asking about his religion; he is Irish, that is enough. We may not agree with his religion, but it matters not; his feelings go deeper than any religion. You should be aware that he is emotional, kindly and sympathetic. If he is chosen as a juror, his imagination will place him in the dock; really, he is trying himself. You would be guilty of malpractice if you got rid of him, except for the strongest reasons.

An Englishman is not as good as an Irishman, but still, he has come through a long tradition of individual rights, and is not afraid to stand alone; in fact, he is never sure that he is right unless the great majority is against him. The German is not so keen about individual rights except where they concern his own way of life; liberty is not a theory, it is a way of living. Still, he wants to do what is right, and he is not afraid. He has not been among us long, his ways are fixed by his race, his habits are still in the making. We need inquire no further. If he is a Catholic, then he loves music and art; he must be emotional, and will want to help you; give him a chance.

If a Presbyterian enters the jury box and carefully rolls up his umbrella, and calmly and critically sits down, let him go. He is cold as the grave; he knows right from wrong, although he seldom finds anything right. He believes in John Calvin and eternal punishment. Get rid of him with the fewest possible words before he contaminates the others; unless you and your clients are Presbyterians you probably are a bad lot, and even though you may be a Presbyterian, your client most likely is guilty.

If possible, the Baptists are more hopeless than the Presbyterians. They, too, are apt to think that the real home of all outsiders is Sheol, and you do not want them on the jury, and the sooner they leave the better.

The Methodists are worth considering; they are nearer the soil. Their religious emotions can be transmuted into love and charity. They are not half bad; even though they will not take a drink, they really do not need it so much as some of their competitors for their seat next to the throne. If chance sets you down between a Methodist and a Baptist, you will move toward the Methodist to keep warm.

Beware of the Lutherans, especially the Scandinavians; they are almost always sure to convict. Either a Lutheran or Scandinavian is unsafe, but if both in one, plead your client guilty and go down the docket. He learns about sinning and punishing from the preacher, and dares not doubt. A person who disobeys must be sent to hell; he has God's word for that.

As to Unitarians, Universalists, Congregationalists, Jews and other agnostics, don't ask them too many questions; keep them anyhow, especially Jews and agnostics. It is best to inspect a Unitarian, or a Universalist, or a Congregationalist with some care, for they may be prohibitionists; but never the Jews and the real agnostics! And do not, please, accept a prohibitionist; he is too solemn and holy and dyspeptic. He knows your client would not have been indicted unless he were a drinking man, and anyone who drinks is guilty of something, probably much worse than he is charged with, although it is not set out in the indictment. Neither would he have employed *you* as his lawyer had he not been guilty.

I have never experimented with Christian Scientists; they are much too serious for me. Somehow, solemn people seem to think that pleasure is wicked. Only the gloomy and dyspeptic can be trusted to convict. Shakespeare knew: "Yon Cassius has a lean and hungry look; he thinks too much; such men are dangerous." You may defy all the rest of the rules if you can get a man who laughs. Few things in this world are of enough importance to warrant considering them seriously. So, by all means, choose a man who laughs. A juror who laughs hates to find anyone guilty.

Never take a wealthy man on a jury. He will convict, unless the defendant is accused of violating the anti-trust law, selling worthless stocks or bonds, or something of that kind. Next to the Board of Trade, for him, the penitentiary is the most important of all public buildings. These imposing structures stand for capitalism. Civilization could not possibly exist without them. Don't take a man because he is a "good" man; this means nothing. You should find out what he is good *for*. Neither should a man be accepted because he is a bad sort. There are too many ways of being good or bad. If you are defending, you want imaginative individuals. You are not interested in the morals of the juror. If a man is instinctively kind and sympathetic, take him.

Then, too, there are the women. These are now in the jury box. A new broom sweeps clean. It leaves no speck on the floor or under the bed, or in the darkest corner of life. To these new jurors, the welfare of the state depends on the verdict. It will be so for many years to come. The chances are that it would not have made the slightest difference to the state if all cases had been decided the other way. It might, however, make a vast difference to the unfortunates facing cruel, narrow-minded jurors who pass judgment on their fellow-men. To the defendants it might have meant the fate of life rather than death.

But what is one life more or less in the general spawning? It may float away on the tide, or drop to the depths of oblivion, broken, crushed and dead. The great sea is full of embryo lives ready to take the places of those who have gone before. One more unfortunate lives and dies as the endless stream flows on, and little it matters to the wise judges who coldly pronounce long strings of words in droning cadence; the victims are removed, they come and go, and the judges keep on chanting senseless phrases laden with doom upon the bowed heads of those before them. The judge is as unconcerned about the actual meaning of it all as the soughing wind rustling the leaves of a tree just outside the courthouse door.

Women still take their new privilege seriously. They are all puffed up with the importance of the part they feel they play, and are sure they represent a great step forward in the world. They believe that the sex is co-operating in a great cause. Like the rest of us, they do not know which way is forward and which is backward, or whether either one is any way at all. Luckily, as I feel, my services were almost over when women invaded the jury box.

A few years ago I became interested in a man charged with selling some brand of intoxicant in a denatured land that needed cheering. I do not know whether he sold it or not. I forgot to ask him. I viewed the case with mixed feelings of pity and contempt, for as Omar philosophized, "I wonder often what the vintners buy one-half so precious as the stuff they sell." When I arrived on the scene, the courtroom looked ominous with women jurors. I managed to get rid of all but two, while the dismissed women lingered around in the big room waiting for the victory, wearing solemn faces and white ribbons. The jury disagreed. In the second trial there were four women who would not budge from their seats or their verdict. Once more I went back to the case with distrust and apprehension. The number of women in the jury box had grown to six. All of them were unprejudiced. They said so. But everyone connected with the case was growing tired and skeptical, so we concluded to call it a draw. This was my last experience with women jurors. I formed a fixed opinion that they were absolutely dependable, but I did not want them.

Whether a jury is a good one or a bad one depends on the point of view. I have always been an attorney for the defense. I can think of nothing, not even war, that has brought so much misery to the human race as prisons. And all of it so futile!

I once spent a winter on the shores of the Mediterranean Sea. In front of my windows, four fishermen were often wearily trudging back and forth, and slowly dragging a long net across the sand. When it was safely landed, a few small flopping fish disclosed the results of their labors. These were scattered dying on the beach, while the really worth-while fishes were left in the sea. It somehow reminded me of our courts and juries, and other aims and efforts of optimistic men, and their idle undertakings and disheartening results.

Judges and jurors are like the rest of humans. Now and then some outstanding figures will roll up their sleeves, as it were, and vigorously set to work to reform the courts and get an efficient administration of justice. This will be ably seconded by the newspapers, lashing courts and jurors, past, present and prospective, into a spasm of virtue that brings down the innocent and guilty together, assuming always that there are innocent and guilty. Then from a time, every defendant is convicted; and soon the campaign reaches the courts; after ruining a few lives and reputations, the frenzy is over, and life goes on smoothly and tranquilly as before.

When I was a boy in the country, one of the standard occupations was whittling. It became as mechanical as breathing. Since then I have decided that this is as good a way to live as any other. Life depends on the automatic taking in and letting out of breath, but in no way is it lengthened or made happier by deep thinking or wise acting. The one big word that stands over courts and other human activities is FUTILITY.

The courts may be unavailing, lawyers stupid, and both as dry as dust, but the combination makes for something interesting and exciting, and it opens avenues that seem to lead somewhere. Liberty, lives, fortunes often are at stake, and appeals for assistance and mercy lend the air for those who care to hear. In an effort to help, often a casual remark may determine a seemingly vital situation, when perhaps the remark, of all the palaver, was the least important one breathed forth. In all questions men are frequently influenced by some statement which, spoken at the eventful time, determines fate. The most unforeseen, accidental meetings sometimes result in seemingly new and strangely fateful family lines. In fact, all that occurs in life is an endless sequence of events resulting from the wildest chance.

Amongst the twelve in a jury box are all degrees of alertness, all sorts of ideas, and a variety of emotions; and the lawyers, too, are important factors in the outcome. They are closely observed by the jurors. They are liked or disliked; mayhap because of what they say, or how they speak, or pronounce their words, or part their hair. It may be that a lawyer is disliked because he talks too little or too much, more often the latter. But a lawyer of subtlety should know when to stop, and when to go on, and how far to go. As a rule, he must not seem to be above the juror, nor below him. He must not too obviously strive for effect. He often meets baffling situations not easily explained. Sometimes it is better for him to talk of something else. Explanations must not be too fantastic or ridiculous. It does no harm to admit the difficulty of the situation, to acknowledge that this circumstance or that seems against him. Many facts point to guilt, but in another light these facts may appear harmless.

Lawyers are apt to interpret deeds and motives as they wish them to appear. As a matter of fact, most actions are subject to various inferences, sometimes quite improbable, but nonetheless true. Identifications show common examples of mistakes. Many men are in prison and some are sent to death through mistaken identifications. One needs but recall the countless errors he himself has made. How many have met some person whom they believed to be an old-time friend, and have found themselves greeting a total stranger? This is a common mistake made in restaurants and other public places. Many identifications in court are made from having seen a person but once, and under conditions not critical. Many are made from descriptions and photographs, and urged on by detectives, lawyers, and other vitally interested in the results. From all of this it is easy to see that many are convicted who are guiltless of crime. In situations of strong agitation, acquittals are rare, and sentences made long and barbarous and inhuman.

The judge is, of course, an important part of the machinery and administration of the court. Like carpenters and lawyers, brick-layers and saloon-keepers, they are not all alike. No two of them have the same fitness for their positions. No two have the same education; not two have the same natural understanding of themselves and their fellow-man, or are gifted with the same discernment and balance.

Not that judges are lacking in knowledge of law. The ordinary rules for the administration of law are rather simple and not difficult to follow. But judges should be students of life, even more than of law. Biology and psychology, which form the basis of understanding human conduct, should be taken into account. Without a fair knowledge of the mechanism of man, and the motives and urges that govern his life, it is idle to venture to fathom a situation; but with some knowledge, officers and the public can be most useful in preserving and protecting those who most need such help. The life of almost any unfortunate, if rightly understood, can be readjusted to some plan of order and system, instead of left to drift on to ruin, the victim of ignorance, hatred and chance.

If the physician so completely ignored natural causes as the lawyers and judges, the treatment of disease would be relegated to witchcraft and magic, and the dungeon and rack would once more hold high carnival in driving devils out of sick and afflicted. Many of the incurable victims of crime are like those who once were incurable victims of disease; they are the product of vicious and incompetent soothsayers who control their destinies.

Every human being, whether parent, teacher, physician, or prosecutor, should make the comfort and happiness of their dependents their first concern. Now and then some learned courts take a big view of life, but scarcely do they make an impression until some public brainstorm drives them back in their treatment of crime to the methods of sorcery and conjury.

No scientific attitude toward crime can be adopted until lawyers, like physicians and scientists, recognize that cause and effect determine the conduct of men.

When lawyers and courts, and laymen, accept the scientific theory which the physicians forced upon the world long years ago, then men will examine each so-called delinquency until they discover its cause, and then learn how to remove the cause. This requires sympathy, humanity, love of one's fellow-man, and a strong faith in the power of knowledge and experience to conquer the maladies of men. The forum of the lawyers may then grow smaller, the courthouse may lose its spell, but the world will profit a thousandfold by a kindlier and more understanding relation toward all humankind.

Jury Selection in
State of Tennessee v. John Thomas Scopes,
a/k/a "The Monkey Trial"

No. 20, J. P. Massingill, duly sworn by the court and examined on his voir dire, testified as follows:

Questions by the Court:

- Q: Have you formed or expressed an opinion as to the guilt or innocence of the defendant in this case?
- A: From rumors and newspapers—of course, I read. I don't know anything about the evidence.
- Q: You haven't talked with any person who professed to know the facts?
- A: No, sir.
- Q: Now, Mr. Massingill, could you go into the jury box and wholly disregard any impression or opinion you have?
- A: Yes, Sir.
- Q: And try the case wholly on the law and the evidence, rendering a fair and impartial verdict to both sides?
- A: I think so; yes, Sir.

Court: He seems to be competent, gentlemen.
Mr. McKenzie: Pass him to you, Colonel.

Questions by Mr. Darrow:

Q: What is your business?
A: I am a minister.
Q: Whereabouts?
A: I live in Rhea County.
Q: Where do you preach?
A: I preach over the county in the rural sections.
Q: You mean you haven't any regular church?
A: I have. I am pastoring four churches—have four appointments.
Q: Ever preach on evolution?
A: I don't think so, definitely; that is, on evolution alone.
Q: Did you ever preach on evolution?
A: Yes. I haven't as a subject; just taken that up; in connection with other subjects. I have referred to it in discussing it.
Q: Against it or for it?
A: I am strictly for the Bible.
Q: I am talking about evolution. I am not talking about the Bible. Did you preach for or against evolution?
A: Is that a fair question, Judge?

Court: Yes, answer the question.

A: Well, I preached against it, of course! (Applause).
Q: Why, "of course?"

Court: Let's have order.
Mr. Darrow: Your honor, I am going to ask to have anybody excluded that applauds.
Court: Yes, if you repeat that, ladies and gentlemen, you will be excluded. We cannot have applause. If you have any feeling in this case you must not express it in the courthouse, so don't repeat the applause. If you do, I will have to exclude you.

Q: You have a very firm conviction—a very strong opinion against evolution, haven't you?
A: Well, some points in evolution.
Q: Are you trying to get on this jury?
A: No, sir.
Q: Have you formed a strong conviction against evolution?
A: Well, I have.

Q: You think you would be a fair juror in this case?
A: Well, I can take the law and the evidence in the case, I think, and try a man right.
Q: I asked if you think you thought you could be a fair juror?
A: Yes, sir.
Q: You have heard that he is an evolutionist, haven't you?
A: Yes, sir, I have heard that.
Q: And in your opinion he has been teaching contrary to the Bible?

General Stewart: If your honor please, I except to that. The question involved here will be whether or not—not, I apprehend if Mr. Scopes taught anything that is contrary to the Bible—that isn't the question. He has asked him whether or not he has prejudged the guilt of the defendant.
Court: He has a right to know that.
General Stewart: The man has already stated to him that he had no opinion in the case.
Mr. Darrow: Do you think he would be a fair juror in the case?
General Stewart: Yes, I do, if he says so.
Mr. Darrow: I don't.
Court: I think the lawyers have the right to get all the information they can on the subject, and I will treat both sides alike.
Court: Questions by the court:

Q: Have you, in your mind now, Mr. Massingill, a fixed opinion that he has taught a theory contrary to the theory of the Bible as to the creation of man?
A: Yes, sir.
Q: Would that have any weight with you or any bearing with you in the trial of this case if you were selected as a juror?
A: I think I am fair and honest enough to lay aside things and give a man justice.

Court: You may proceed, gentlemen. He seems to be competent.
Mr. Darrow: You now have an opinion that evolution is contrary to the Bible and that my client has been teaching evolution; as you stand there now, that is your opinion?

A: From the information I have in regard to his teaching.
Q: That is your opinion now, isn't it, as you stand there now?
A: Sure it is.
Q: You could change it if you heard evidence enough to change it on?
A: Yes, sir.
Q: Otherwise you couldn't?
A: I have no right to; I don't think.

Mr. Darrow: I challenge for cause.
Court: Well, I want every juror to start in with an open mind. I will excuse you, Mr. Massingill. . . .

[The Prosecution rejects a juror]

Venireman J. T. Leuty was duly sworn and replied as follows to questions asked by the court:

> **Q:** Have you formed or expressed an opinion as to the guilt or innocence of this defendant?
> **A:** No, sir.
> **Q:** If chosen on the jury, could you go into the box without prejudice or bias either way, and try the case on the law and the evidence?
> **A:** Yes, sir.

Court: He is a competent juror.

Examination by **J. G. McKenzie:**

> **Q:** Mr. Leuty, you say you have been hearing about this case?
> **A:** No, sir, just talk.
> **Q:** When he was arrested?
> **A:** Yes, sir.
> **Q:** And, of course, everybody formed an opinion, and naturally would? That's right?
> **A:** No, sir; I didn't hear any evidence in this case, and didn't form any opinion at all.
> **Q:** You didn't form any opinion from what you heard other people say?
> **A:** No, sir.
> **Q:** And haven't an opinion now?
> **A:** No, sir.

Mr. J. G. McKenzie—We pass him to you.

Examination by **Mr. Darrow:**

> **Q:** Have you ever been a member of a church?
> **A:** No, sir.
> **Q:** How long have you lived here?
> **A:** All my life.
> **Q:** What is your business?
> **A:** Well, I am a kind of a farmer now.
> **Q:** Here in Dayton?
> **A:** No, sir; I live in Rhea Springs.
> **Q:** That is in this county?
> **A:** Yes, sir.
> **Q:** You have never studied evolution?
> **A:** No, sir.

Q: Are you much of a reader?
A: I read some. I used to read a great deal.
Q: Books?
A: Yes, and magazines and newspapers. Used to read books.
Q: You used to read books. And you went to school here, I suppose, rather than where you live now?
A: I went to the public schools in Rhea County.
Q: Did you ever hear anybody talk about evolution?
A: Oh, well, I have heard it talked about when they got this question up.
Q: They never talked about it before down here, did they?.
A: Well, they might in a general way, but people never paid much attention to it.
Q: You have not any prejudice against the doctrine or idea of evolution?
A: No, sir.
Q: You don't know what your neighbors think about this case?
A: I suppose some of them have thought about it.
Q: You wouldn't care what they thought if you were on this jury?
A: No, it wouldn't make any difference to me if I was on this jury.
Q: If you were on this jury it would not make any difference to you what your neighbors thought?
A: No, sir.

Mr. J. G. McKenzie—Challenge by the state.
The Court: Mr. Leuty, we will excuse you.
Mr. Darrow: Have they got a right to do that?
The Court Colonel, perhaps you don't understand our practice.
The Court: They examine a juror. They pass him to you, and you can examine him and say that you pass him back; then they have the right to challenge him. They have a right to pass him back and then you take him or reject him. That is our practice.
Mr. Darrow: I thought they were trying to put something over on us.
The Court: No, if they tried to I would not let them.
Mr. Darrow: Don't let them.

It can be quite helpful, when permitted, to have a juror questionnaire for perspective jurors to fill out ahead of trial. Jurors will often answer questions in writing that they will not speak up to in a full courtroom. The disadvantage is that you do not get to see them speak their answers and watch their body movements and expressions.

I always tell jurors in voir dire that I am about to ask them questions the answers to which would be none of my business if I met them in another setting. I tell them, however, that in order to pick the fairest possible jury we must ask them questions which are personal in nature.

If financially available, I would also encourage some of the very best jury experts around the country who can put together a representative mock jury whose deliberations you can view and have videotaped for later analysis as well.

VOIR DIRE

I. INTRODUCTIONS

_____ , Attorney

_____ , Attorney

Name of Client: _____

Family:

_____ Wife

_____ Daughter

_____ Son

II. EXPLAIN VOIR DIRE PROCESS

III. PRIOR JURY EXPERIENCE
    A. Criminal _____ Foreman? _____
       Number of cases _____
       Verdict _____

    B. Civil _____ Foreman? _____

IV. CONSTITUTIONAL RIGHTS
    A. Presumption of innocence

    B. Defendant not required to put on proof

    C. Defendant not required to testify

    D. State has burden of proof—beyond a reasonable doubt

V. BIOGRAPHICAL
    A. PERSONAL

        1. Name: _____
        2. Marital Status: _____
        3. Number of Children: _____
        4. Ages: _____
        5. Address: _____
        6. Community: _____

7. How long have you been a resident of that community: _____
8. Place of birth: _____
9. Have you lived in any other states: _____
10. Have you lived in any other country: _____
    Where: _____
    When: _____
11. What is your approximate annual income: ;_____
    $20,000 or under _____ $20,000 to $40,000 _____
    $40,000 to $75,000 _____   Over $75,000 _____
12. What is your family's combined approximate annual income:
    $20,000 or under _____ $20,000 to $40,000 _____
    $40,000 to $75,000 _____   Over $75,000 _____
13. Do any of you own stocks or bonds: _____
14. Do any of you own a mutual fund: _____
15. Do you file your income taxes on the IRS short form or on the IRS itemized long form: _____
16. Have you or any member of your family ever been audited by the IRS: _____
17. Has any close friend or associate of yours been audited by the IRS:
18. How many automobiles are registered to your household: _____
19. Do you have any bumper stickers on any of those automobiles: _____
    If so, what do they say: _____
20. Have you or any member of your family ever been employed or sought employment by any government agency: _____
    If so, which agency: _____
    If so, how long were you employed: _____
21. Has any close friend of yours ever sought employment or been employed by a government agency: _____
    If so, which agency: _____
    If so, for how long: _____
22. Have you or any member of your family ever required a security clearance for your particular job: _____
    If so, did you receive that security clearance: _____
23. In doing your job, how important is it for you to rely on the judgment of others:
    Very Important _____   Somewhat Important _____
    Not Very Important _____
24. In your job do you have any authority over promotions or over the hiring or firing of other individuals: _____
25. In your job do you have any management responsibilities: _____
    If yes, please explain: _____
26. Are you salaried or an hourly employee or do you work on a commission or are you self employed: _____

B. OCCUPATION
1. Where do you work: _____
2. How long have you been employed there: _____
3. Duties: _____
   _____
4. Do you supervise any individuals: _____
   If so, how many: _____

C. EDUCATION
1. How far did you go in school: _____
2. Did you go to college: _____
   If so, name of college: _____
3. What was your major at college: _____
4. Did you belong to any clubs or activities while at school: ____
5. Did you participate in any sports while at school: _____
6. Did you graduate from high school: _____
7. Did you graduate from college: _____

D. CLUBS
1. Did you belong to any organizations as a youngster: _____
2. Do you belong to any social or civic clubs presently: _____
3. If so, do you hold any office: _____
4. How long have you belonged to these social clubs: _____
5. How frequently do you attend meetings: _____
6. Do you belong to or support in any way any environmental group or cause. If so, what group and how? _____

E. POLITICS
1. Do you belong to any particular political party: _____
2. Do you find yourself voting for one particular party more than another: _____
3. Do you vote in every election: _____ Most elections: _____
   Few elections: _____ No elections at all: _____
4. Have you ever held any political office: _____
5. Have you ever run a campaign for a political office: _____
6. Have you ever heard that you were being considered as a candidate to be appointed to a political office: _____
7. Have you ever held any political office within a political party, such as precinct chairman, etc.: _____
8. Have you ever been employed by an elected official: _____
   If so, whom: _____
9. Have you ever worked in a political campaign: _____
   If so, for what candidate: _____
10. What office was the candidate running for: _____
11. What political party does he belong to: _____

F. RELIGION
   1. Do you belong to a particular church or synagogue: _____
      If so, name: _____
   2. How long: _____
   3. If not, do you identify with a particular religious denomination: _____
   4. Do you attend services: _____
   5. How frequently: _____
   6. Do you hold an office in that particular church or synagogue: _____
   7. If not now, have you ever held office in that particular church or synagogue: _____

G. MILITARY SERVICE
   1. Have any of you served in the military: _____
      If so, what branch: _____
   2. When: _____
   3. What rank did you hold: _____
   4. Where were you stationed: _____
   5. Did you see military combat _____
      If so, where: _____
      When: _____
   6. What type of discharge did you receive: _____
   7. Were you ever injured in military service: _____
   8. Were you ever forced to injure anyone else in the course of military service: _____
   9. Did you ever have occasion to order anyone else into combat: _____

H. RECREATION
   1. Do you hunt: _____
      If so, with what kind of weapon: _____
   2. If so, what kind of game do you hunt: _____
   3. If so, how frequently: _____
   4. Do you fish: _____
   5. If so, do you keep your catch: _____
   6. What other recreational activities do you participate in: _____
   7. How frequently: _____
   8. Do you boat? _____ Where? _____
      What kind of boat? _____

I. WEAPONS
   1. Do you own any firearms: _____
      If so, what types: _____
   2. If so, for what purpose: _____

3. If so, how frequently do you fire them: _____
4. If so, how adept are you at discharging them: _____
5. Do you own any knives: _____
6. If so, how many: _____
7. If so, for what purpose: _____

J. LAW ENFORCEMENT
   1. Have any of you or any member of your family been employed in a law enforcement type job: _____
      If so, please explain: _____
   2. Have any close friends of yours been employed in a law enforcement type job: _____
   3. Have you or any member of your family been employed as a security guard: _____
   4. Has any close friend of yours been employed as a security guard: _____
   5. Do you believe that a law enforcement officer's testimony should be given more weight because he is a law enforcement officer: _____
   6. Have you ever been arrested: _____
   7. Have you ever been stopped by a police officer: _____
   8. Have you ever been investigated by a police officer: _____
   9. Have you ever been questioned by a police officer: _____
   10. Have you ever been charged with a crime: _____
   11. Have you ever been a witness to a crime: _____
   12. Have you or any member of your family ever been a victim of a crime: _____
   13. Has any close personal friend ever been a victim of a crime: _____
   14. If so, did you sustain property loss: _____
   15. If so, did you sustain personal injury: _____
   16. If so, was an individual arrested: _____
   17. If so, was the individual prosecuted: _____
   18. If so, were you the prosecutor in the case: _____
   19. If so, did you or any member of your family have to testify in the case: _____
   20. Did the case go to trial: _____
   21. Was the individual convicted for the offense charged: _____
   22. Was the individual convicted of another offense: _____
   23. Was the individual acquitted: _____

K. ENTERTAINMENT
   1. Do you watch television: _____
   2. Approximately how many hours a day would you watch television: _____

3. What are your favorite television programs: _____
4. Do you have cable television: _____
   If so, to which pay stations do you subscribe: _____
5. Do you have a satellite dish: _____
6. Do you own a VCR or DVD Player: _____
7. If so, what are your favorite movies that you rent: _____
8. Do you watch television while eating dinner: _____
9. Do you watch news programs on television: _____
10. If so, which news programs do you prefer: _____
11. Do you go to the movie theater: _____
    If so, what are your favorite movies: _____
    If so, how frequently do you go to the movies: _____
    If so, who do you go to the movies with: _____
    If so, what kind of movies do you prefer: _____
    Suspense _____   Romance _____   Comedies _____
    Horror _____   Western _____   Science Fiction _____
    Police _____   Other _____
12. Do you attend other theatrical events such as :
    Symphony Concerts _____   Rock Concerts _____
    Theatrical Productions _____   Ballet _____
    Other Dance _____
13. Do any of you visit museums: _____
    If so, what kinds of museums: _____
14. What kind of music do you prefer: _____
15. Do you listen to the radio: _____
    If so, is there a particular radio station that you prefer: _____
16. Do you buy records, cassettes, or compact disks: _____
    If so, which do you prefer: _____
    If so, which types of music do you prefer: _____
17. Do you or any member of your family own a stereo at home: _____
    If so, what is the approximate value of your stereo: _____
18. Do any of you play a musical instrument: _____
    If so, which instrument: _____
19. Do any of you read books: _____
    If so, how frequently: _____
    If so, what are some of your favorite books: _____
    What kinds of books do you prefer: _____
20. Do any of you read magazines: _____
    If so, what kinds of magazines: _____
    If so, how frequently do you read magazines: _____

21. Do any of you read newspapers: _____
    If so, which newspapers: _____
    If so, how frequently do you read the newspapers: _____
22. Do you believe what you read in the newspaper: _____

L. HEALTH
   1. Do any of you have any health problems: _____
   2. Does any member of your family have a health problem: ____
   3. Would your health problem cause you difficulties in serving as a juror in this case: _____
   4. Would your family member's health problem cause you difficulty in serving as a juror in this case: _____

M. ENVIRONMENTAL LAWS

(Please circle response)

   1. Do you feel that our environmental laws are:
      A. Too lenient
      B. Too harsh
      C. Just about right

   2. Do you feel that there are too many environmental regulations?

   3. In dealing with governmental Bureaucracy, do you feel such dealings are:
      A. Too easy
      B. Too hard
      C. Just about right

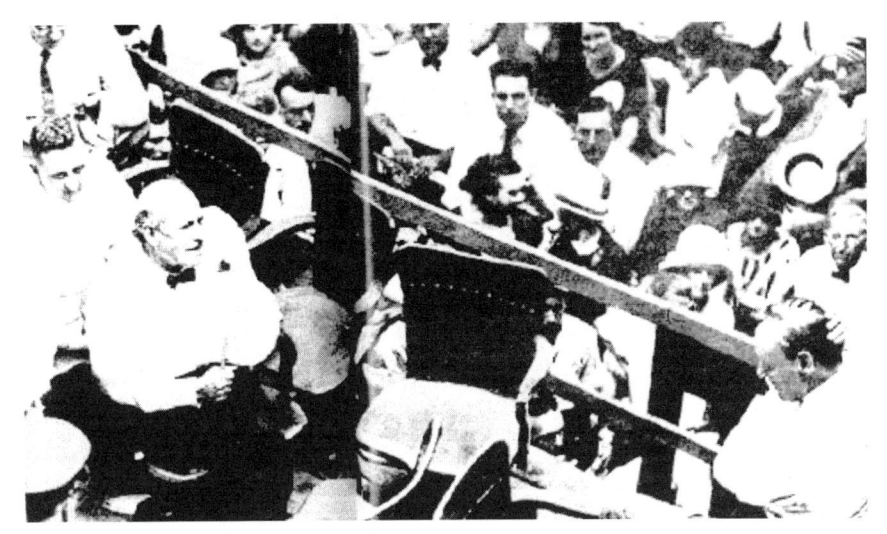

Darrow examines William Jennings Bryan

CHAPTER 2

CROSS-EXAMINING THE EXPERT

"A courtroom is not a place where truth and innocence inevitably triumph; it is only an arena where contending lawyers fight not for justice, but to win."
                                                                Clarence Darrow

Everyone has his own bible. There is no better way to cross-examine any witness than with his bible. Clarence Darrow proved that when he devastated William Jennings Bryan in the *Scopes* trial by cross-examining him with the Bible. Darrow called Bryan to the stand and began to ask him questions about his Bible. The following cross-examination left Bryan a broken man. He died five days after the trial.

DARROW: Do you believe Joshua made the sun stand still?
BRYAN: I believe what the Bible says.
DARROW: I suppose you mean the earth stood still?
BRYAN: I don't know. I am talking about the Bible now. I accept the Bible absolutely.
DARROW: Do you believe at the time the entire sun went around the earth?
BRYAN: No. I believe the earth goes around the sun.
DARROW: Do you believe that the men who wrote it thought that the day could be lengthened or that sun could be stopped?

BRYAN: I believe what they wrote was inspired by the Almighty. He may have used language that could be understood at that time–instead of language that could not be understood until Darrow was born.

DARROW: No, Mr. Bryan, have you ever pondered what would have happened to the earth if it stood still suddenly?

BRYAN: No.

DARROW: Don't you know it would have been converted into a molten mass of matter?

BRYAN: You testify to that when you get on the stand. I will give you a chance.

DARROW: You believe the story of the flood to be a literal interpretation?

BRYAN: Yes sir.

DARROW: When was the flood?

BRYAN: I would not attempt to fix the day.

DARROW: But you do think that the Bible itself says? Don't you know how it was arrived at?

BRYAN: I never made a calculation.

DARROW: What do you think?

BRYAN: I do not think about things I don't think about.

DARROW: Do you think about things you do think about?

BRYAN: Well sometimes.

Bryan left the stand a broken man. It was truly a killer cross-examination.

We, too have access to the bible of government witnesses in environmental criminal cases. Any government witness who is engaged in sampling and sampling analysis of "hazardous wastes" uses the Environmental Protection Agency's (EPA) bible, S.W.-846, which is the gospel according to the EPA when it comes to sampling and sampling analysis. It is a government document and is available from the Government Printing Office. S.W.-846 consists of four volumes. Volumes IA, IB and IC discusses laboratory analysis, and Volume II discusses sampling collection and analysis in the field. It is a loose leaf document which is updated periodically and is ripe with jewels for cross-examination.

In beginning to prepare for cross-examination, you need to thoroughly familiarize yourself with S.W.-846. The following are some areas at which you should take a particularly careful look when preparing to undertake the cross-examination.

Sampling Plan

S.W.-846 at Section 9.2.2 says that the sampling plan is usually a written document "that describes the objectives and details the individual tasks of the sampling effort and how they will be performed." Many times samplers will not have a written sampling plan. The lack of a sampling plan shows at the very least sloppy work and may show complete disregard for the teachings of the sampler's bible, S.W.-846. As the bible states, "the more detailed the sampling plan, the less opportunity for oversight or misunderstanding during sampling, analysis and data treatment." S.W.-846 § 9.2.2.

S.W.-846 recommends that several experienced personnel be assigned specific tasks. There should be an end-user of the data, "who will be using the data to obtain program objectives and thus will be best prepared that the data objectives are understood and incorporated into the sampling plan." You need to find out who that person is and what his participation was, if any, in the compilation and writing of the sampling plan. The sampling plan should include an experienced member of the field team who will actually be hands on. Find out who that person is and what his involvement was.

An analytic chemist should be involved "because the analytical requirements for sampling preservation and holding times will be factors around which the sampling plan will be written." *Id.* S.W.-846 recommends that an engineer should be involved when a complex manufacturing process is being sampled. Who is that person? What are his qualifications? What involvement did he have in writing the sampling plan?

The statistician, who will review the approach and verify the data, should be involved. Again, who is he, what was his involvement and qualifications? Most importantly, a quality assurance representative should be involved. He will determine the number of blanks, duplicates, spike samples and other steps required to document the accuracy and precision of the resulting data base. You will probably find that in most sampling projects, no quality assurance representative was involved at any stage. You may also find that such quality assurance methods such as spikes, duplicate and field samples were not used. S.W.-846 fully discusses the importance of these quality assurance methods in order to insure the accuracy of the analysis. When a sampling project does not include the above personnel and does not include the very important quality assurance methods, the court may look hard at suppressing the evidence and certainly the jury will examine thoroughly the reliability of the results.

Decontamination

Every sampling plan should include a very extensive decontamination plan. Again, this plan should be written. Without proper steps for decontamination, the sampling analysis not only will be tainted but may be absolutely worthless as evidence. You need to find out what decontamination zone was set up so that persons going on the "hot or exclusion zone" where the sampling is actually occurring do not bring with them materials that could contaminate the samples. Find out what training in decontamination the sampling personnel have had. Find out where their equipment came from. If they are wearing level B protective gear or "moon-suits," find out if they have been used before. Have the boots and gloves been used before? If so, how, when, and by whom were they decontaminated? If they are new, what laboratory has insured that they are completely free of contamination and what process was involved to insure that?

Look carefully at the sampling tools that were involved. If they were used, how, when and by whom were they decontaminated? What quality assurance procedures were used on site to make sure that the tools did not bring any substances with them into the sampling zone? If the tools are new, what laboratory has insured that they are free of contamination and what process was involved? Look carefully at the sampling jars. If they have been used before, when, by whom and what process was used to clean them and make them free from contamination? If they are new, what laboratory has supplied them and has assured that they are free of contamination? What process did they use?

What personnel were allowed in to the "hot or exclusion zone" who were not involved in the sampling and who may have not been trained as to the sampling plan? What personnel were involved in the sampling who were not themselves trained in the decontamination plan?

What steps were made to decontaminate clothing, tools, sample jars, equipment and personnel when they left the sampling or "hot or exclusion zones?" Even though failure to decontaminate at that point may not effect the quality of the actual sample, such failure to decontaminate makes a great jury argument that if these substances are so hazardous, why aren't personnel who have been handling them throwing away tools and clothing. Why are they simply storing these items without decontaminating them for future sampling?

Health & Safety

S.W.-846 recommends that a comprehensive health and safety plan be involved. You need to find out if the personnel doing the sampling have met the basic OSHA 40–hour training requirement. Is there a written health and safety plan? Does it discuss what materials are on site and what dangers are involved with those materials? Is there a nearby hospital contact who has been briefed on possible emergencies? Find out who that person is and what he has been told. Find out if the level of protective gear used on site was really necessary or whether it was done to merely enhance the hazardous nature of the sampling for video presentation.

Sampling Tools and Methods

You need to find out what sampling tools were used and whether they are the tools recommended by S.W.-846. For instance, many of the cases we encounter involve the storage of materials in 55–gallon drums. The 55–gallon drums are 34 inches high. You will often run into samplings by EPA and other authorities where tools are used such as scoops. A typical scoop is about 13 inches long. Obviously a 13–inch scoop when put into a 34–inch drum will only yield a sample from the top of the drum. S.W.-846 recommends a series of tools depending on the consistency of the material. For instance, for sludge S.W.-846 recommends a trier. S.W.-846 § 9.5.5. A trier is 36 inches long and will yield a complete vertical sample of the material. An illustration of the trier can be found on the next page.

If the appropriate tools were not used, then representative samples were not taken. If representative samples were not taken, you have a jewel for cross-examination, because the sample may show something very different than what was

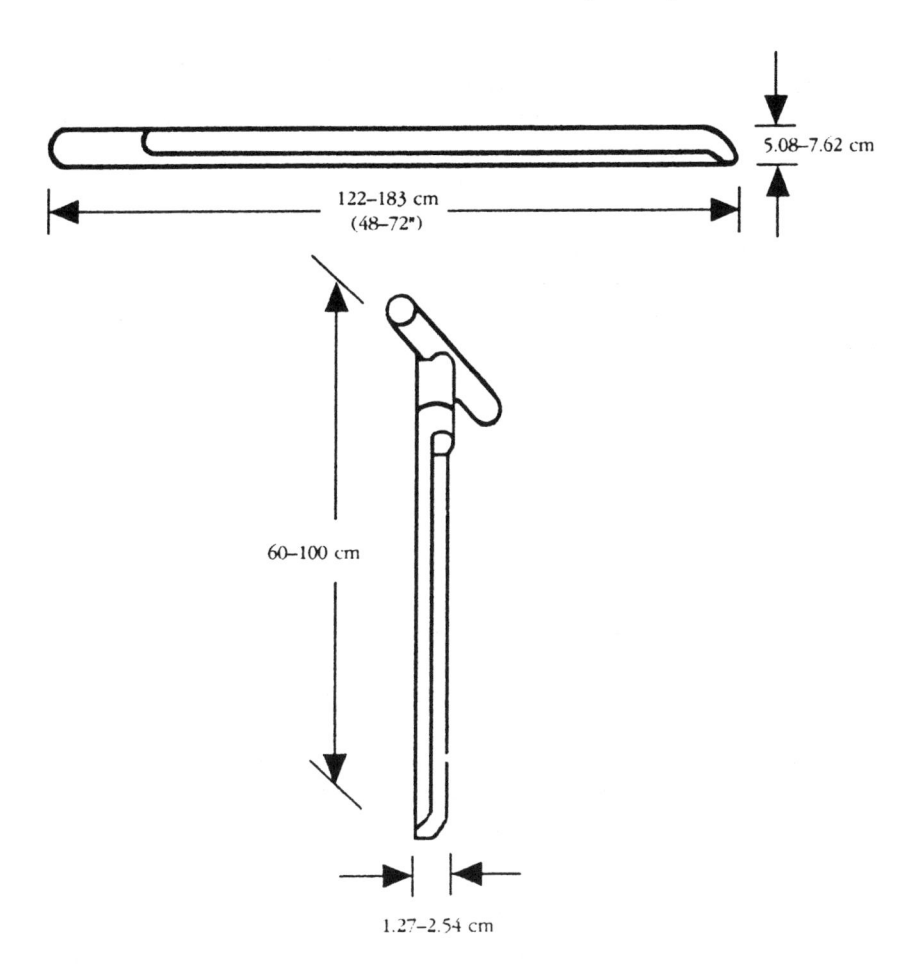

[Figure: dimensions 122–183 cm (48–72"), 5.08–7.62 cm, 60–100 cm, 1.27–2.54 cm]

actually in the drum. S.W.-846 goes on to discuss fully what sample preparation methods should be used before the sample is sealed in the sample jar.

You need to find out if, in fact, the jars were sealed. What was then done with the jars? Who was the custodian of the jars? In what conditions were the jars kept before being delivered to the laboratory? How long were the jars kept before being delivered to the laboratory? Then, of course, what did the laboratory do with the jars and the samples once it received them. What methods were used by the laboratory for analysis of the samples? Were the methods used approved by S.W.-846? What internal paperwork shows the chain of sample as well as its analysis? What does the internal audit say about the laboratory and its quality assurance?

Obtaining the Above Information

Prosecutors will be extremely reluctant to turn over the information discussed above. Two types of motions can be very effective in discovering the information.

First are motions to suppress. If the correct procedures recommended in S.W.-846 are not followed, the court may well suppress the evidence because the reliability of the results cannot be assured. Materials may be contaminated or they may be mixed with other materials. Courts do and have suppressed sample results under these circumstances. At the very least, however, you will get some discovery of the documentation, if any, that the government has as to its sampling and analysis.

The other category of motions that can be very helpful are *Brady* motions. Obviously if correct procedures are not followed, such evidence is exculpatory and is certainly, at the very least, ripe impeachment material for your cross-examination. As such, you need to file very specific *Brady* requests asking for the kinds of documents that S.W.-846 discusses. In environmental cases, I have filed over 30 such specific *Brady* requests in each case. Be sure to ask for everything that might be involved.

Government Teaching Documents

Another jewel in preparing for your cross-examination are those materials relied upon by government witnesses in conducting their own seminars and in-service training. You certainly have a right in any motions hearing to ask for any document that the witness has written or used in teaching a seminar. When examining these documents, you will find obvious prejudices in favor of prosecution and attempts to defeat the defense.

I received a document once entitled *Overview of Sampling* which advised the samplers not to "over-sample." One of the reasons that the author advises against over-sampling is that it may "risk bias in favor of defense." If the reliability of the sampling analysis and quality assurance are the goals, why would anyone want to prevent over-sampling because it may risk bias in favor of the defense? Obviously this author is not seeking the truth but merely a conviction. Courts and juries will be extremely upset when they see such an obvious prejudice and disregard for the truth.

Also, I received a document written by a government environmental enforcement agent which stated "many times what makes good criminal evidence is not adequate for environmental assessments and vice versa." Neither I nor the judge could ever figure out what that meant, but both of us knew we did not like it. Obviously such a statement is a jewel for cross-examination because again it shows the bias against the truth and the favor of prosecuting for conviction.

Setting Up the Cross-Examination

Having thoroughly familiarized yourself with S.W.-846, gathered all documents that exist or do not exist on behalf of the government and their sampling and having closely examined any teaching documents used by the government witnesses, you are ready to set up your cross-examination. Getting a government agent to recognize that S.W.-846 is his bible is relatively easy.

The following is a cross-examination I conducted which shows how easy the allegiance to the bible can be demonstrated:

TRANT: Mr. Kleinhenz did you have a written sampling plan to go by when you went out to the site on the 21st or March 5th?
KLEINHENZ: No, we don't have written sampling plans. We don't use them.
TRANT: You are familiar with S.W.-846 are you not?
KLEINHENZ: Sure.
TRANT: And that's–what is that?
KLEINHENZ: That's the federal. U.S.E.P.A. Basically it's our guidance document on sampling as well as sampling analysis.

Having established the witnesses' allegiance to S.W.-846, you can then have a great time and very effectively cross-examine him with the document. My cross-examination of Mr. Kleinhenz went on as follows:

TRANT: And you know that they lay out very definite considerations and recommendations for a sampling plan.
KLEINHENZ: On how to obtain samples, is that correct?
TRANT: Well, also a sampling plan of what you do before you ever get out there, don't they?
KLEINHENZ: They might. I'd have to review that.
TRANT: You're not familiar with that?
KLEINHENZ: Not that particular portion.

(I went on to ask Mr. Kleinhenz about exclusion zones.)

TRANT: And that's why you're supposed to have an exclusion zone that's very highly regulated, marked off, and nobody goes on it except personnel who have been taught about the sampling plan and health and safety plan; isn't that right?
KLEINHENZ: No.
TRANT: You're not suppose to have an exclusion zone?
KLEINHENZ: No, that's not what I'd. . . .
TRANT: Well, what are you telling me then?
KLEINHENZ: Well, I answered your question, the answer to that was no.
TRANT: You're not suppose to have an exclusion zone?
KLEINHENZ: That wasn't your question.
TRANT: Well, I'm asking you that now. Pardon me if I'm dumber than you, but are you suppose to have an exclusion zone?
KLEINHENZ: Yes.
TRANT: And the purpose of that is what?
KLEINHENZ: The purpose of an exclusion zone is to provide safety for the workers on site. You designate a certain area. Inside that you're supposed to wear a certain level of protection. Outside that area you could wear a different level of protection.

TRANT:	But isn't it also to make sure that you maintain quality control. Isn't that another purpose of the exclusion zone.
KLEINHENZ:	It's mainly for the health and safety workers.
TRANT:	I know. You said that.
KLEINHENZ:	Right.
TRANT:	But isn't it also to maintain quality control?
KLEINHENZ:	I'm not sure what you're getting at.
TRANT:	Well, what I'm getting at is, if you have people that haven't been trained in the sampling plan, whatever it is, and the health and safety plan going up on the pads, doesn't that effect your quality control?

Mr. Kleinhenz left the witness stand a broken and incredible witness. Just as Darrow had done with Bryan, he had been impeached with his own bible. You, too, can conduct killer cross-examinations of government scientific witnesses in these cases. I know, because their bible tells me so.

Darrow's examination of William Jennings Bryan

Hays:	The defense desires to call Mr. Bryan as a witness, and, of course, the only question here is whether Mr. Scopes taught what these children said he taught, we recognize what Mr. Bryan says as a witness would not be very valuable. We think there are other questions involved, and we should want to take Mr. Bryan's testimony for the purpose of our record, even if your honor thinks it is not admissible in general, so we wish to call him now.
The Court:	Do you think you have a right to his testimony or evidence like you did these others?
McKenzie:	I don't think it is necessary to call him, calling a lawyer who represents a client.
The Court:	If you ask him about any confidential matter, I will protect him, of course.
Darrow:	On scientific matters, Col. Bryan can speak for himself.
Bryan:	If your honor please, I insist that Mr. Darrow can be put on the stand, and Mr. Malone and Mr. Hays.
The Court:	Call anybody you desire. Ask them any questions you wish.
Bryan:	Then, we will call all three of them.
Darrow:	Not at once?
Bryan:	Where do you want me to sit?
The Court:	Mr. Bryan, you are not objecting to going on the stand?
Bryan:	Not at all.
The Court:	Do you want Mr. Bryan sworn?
Darrow:	No.
Bryan:	I can make affirmation; I can say "So help me God, I will tell the truth."
Darrow:	No, I take it you will tell the truth, Mr. Bryan.

Examination of **W.J. Bryan** by **Clarence Darrow,** of counsel for the defense:

Q: You have given considerable study to the Bible, haven't you, Mr. Bryan?
A: Yes, sir, I have tried to.
Q: Then you have made a general study of it?
A: Yes, I have; I have studied the Bible for about fifty years, or sometime more than that, but, of course, I have studied it more as I have become older than when I was but a boy.
Q: You claim that everything in the Bible should be literally interpreted?
A: I believe everything in the Bible should be accepted as it is given there: some of the Bible is given illustratively. For instance: "Ye are the salt of the earth." I would not insist that man was actually salt, or that he had flesh of salt, but it is used in the sense of salt as saving God's people.
Q: But when you read that Jonah swallowed the whale—or that the whale swallowed Jonah—excuse me please—how do you literally interpret that?
A: When I read that a big fish swallowed Jonah—it does not say whale. . . . That is my recollection of it. A big fish, and I believe it, and I believe in a God who can make a whale and can make a man and make both what He pleases.
Q: Now, you say, the big fish swallowed Jonah, and he there remained how long—three days—and then he spewed him upon the land. You believe that the big fish was made to swallow Jonah?
A: I am not prepared to say that; the Bible merely says it was done.
Q: You don't know whether it was the ordinary run of fish, or made for that purpose?
A: You may guess; you evolutionists guess. . . . .
Q: You are not prepared to say whether that fish was made especially to swallow a man or not?
A: The Bible doesn't say, so I am not prepared to say.
Q: But do you believe He made them—that He made such a fish and that it was big enough to swallow Jonah?
A: Yes, sir. Let me add: One miracle is just as easy to believe as another
Q: Just as hard?
A: It is hard to believe for you, but easy for me. A miracle is a thing performed beyond what man can perform. When you get within the realm of miracles; and it is just as easy to believe the miracle of Jonah as any other miracle in the Bible.
Q: Perfectly easy to believe that Jonah swallowed the whale?
A: If the Bible said so; the Bible doesn't make as extreme statements as evolutionists do. . . .
Q: The Bible says Joshua commanded the sun to stand still for the purpose of lengthening the day, doesn't it, and you believe it?
A: I do.
Q: Do you believe at that time the entire sun went around the earth?
A: No, I believe that the earth goes around the sun.

- **Q:** Do you believe that the men who wrote it thought that the day could be lengthened or that the sun could be stopped?
- **A:** I don't know what they thought.
- **Q:** You don't know?
- **A:** I think they wrote the fact without expressing their own thoughts.
- **Q:** Have you an opinion as to whether or not the men who wrote that thought?

Gen. Stewart: I want to object, your honor; it has gone beyond the pale of any issue that could possibly be injected into this lawsuit, expect by imagination. I do not think the defendant has a right to conduct the examination any further and I ask your honor to exclude it.

The Witness: It seems to me it would be too exacting to confine the defense to the facts; if they are not allowed to get away from the facts, what have they to deal with?

The Court: Mr. Bryan is willing to be examined. Go ahead.

Mr. Darrow: I read that years ago. Can you answer my question directly? If the day was lengthened by stopping either the earth or the sun, it must have been the earth?

- **A:** Well, I should say so.
- **Q:** Now, Mr. Bryan, have you ever pondered what would have happened to the earth if it had stood still?
- **A:** No.
- **Q:** You have not?
- **A:** No; the God I believe in could have taken care of that, Mr. Darrow.
- **Q:** I see. Have you ever pondered what would naturally happen to the earth if it stood still suddenly?
- **A:** No.
- **Q:** Don't you know it would have been converted into molten mass of matter?
- **A:** You testify to that when you get on the stand, I will give you a chance.
- **Q:** Don't you believe it?
- **A:** I would want to hear expert testimony on that.
- **Q:** You have never investigated that subject?
- **A:** I don't think I have ever had the question asked.
- **Q:** Or ever thought of it?
- **A:** I have been too busy on things that I thought were of more importance than that.
- **Q:** You believe the story of the flood to be a literal interpretation?
- **A:** Yes, sir.
- **Q:** When was that Flood?
- **A:** I would not attempt to fix the date. The date is fixed, as suggested this morning.
- **Q:** About 4004 B.C.?
- **A:** That has been the estimate of a man that is accepted today. I would not say it is accurate.

Q: That estimate is printed in the Bible?
A: Everybody knows, at least, I think most of the people know, that was the estimate given.
Q: But what do you think that the Bible, itself says? Don't you know how it was arrived at?
A: I never made a calculation.
Q: A calculation from what?
A: I could not say.
Q: From the generations of man?
A: I would not want to say that.
Q: What do you think?
A: I do not think about things I don't think about.
Q: Do you think about things you do think about?
A: Well, sometimes.

(Laughter in the courtyard.)

Policeman: Let us have order. . . .
Stewart: Your honor, he is perfectly able to take care of this, but we are attaining no evidence. This is not competent evidence.
Witness: These gentlemen have not had much chance—they did not come here to try this case. They came here to try revealed religion. I am here to defend it and they can ask me any question they please.
The Court: All right.

(Applause from the court yard.)

Darrow: Great applause from the bleachers.
Witness: From those whom you call "Yokels."
Darrow: I have never called them yokels.
Witness: That is the ignorance of Tennessee, the bigotry.
Darrow: You mean who are applauding you? (Applause.)
Witness: Those are the people whom you insult.
Darrow: You insult every man of science and learning in the world because he does believe in your fool religion.
The Court: I will not stand for that.
Darrow: For what he is doing?
The Court: I am talking to both of you. . . .

Q: Wait until you get to me. Do you know anything about how many people there were in Egypt 3,500 years ago, or how many people there were in China 5,000 years ago?
A: No.

Q: Have you ever tried to find out?
A: No, sir. You are the first man I ever heard of who has been in interested in it. (Laughter.)
Q: Mr. Bryan, am I the first man you ever heard of who has been interested in the age of human societies and primitive man?
A: You are the first man I ever heard speak of the number of people at those different periods.
Q: Where have you lived all your life?
A: Not near you. (Laughter and applause.)
Q: Nor near anybody of learning?
A: Oh, don't assume you know it all.
Q: Do you know there are thousands of books in our libraries on all those subjects I have been asking you about?
A: I couldn't say, but I will take your word for it. . . .
Q: Have you any idea how old the earth is?
A: No.
Q: The Book you have introduced in evidence tells you, doesn't it?
A: I don't think it does, Mr. Darrow.
Q: Let's see whether it does; is this the one?
A: That is the one, I think.
Q: It says B.C. 4004?
A: That is Bishop Usher's calculation.
Q: That is printed in the Bible you introduced?
A: Yes, sir. . . .
Q: Would you say that the earth was only 4,000 years old?
A: Oh, no; I think it is much older than that.
Q: How much?
A: I couldn't say.
Q: Do you say whether the Bible itself says it is older than that?
A: I don't think it is older or not.
Q: Do you think the earth was made in six days?
A: Not six days of twenty-four hours.
Q: Doesn't it say so?
A: No, sir. . . .

The Court: Are you about through, Mr. Darrow?
Darrow: I want to ask a few more questions about the creation.
The Court: I know. We are going to adjourn when Mr. Bryan comes off the stand for the day. Be very brief, Mr. Darrow. Of course, I believe I will make myself clearer. Of course, it is incompetent testimony before the jury. The only reason I am allowing this to go on at all is that they may have it in the appellate court as showing what the affidavit would be.
Bryan: The reason I am answering is not for the benefit of the superior court. It is to keep these gentlemen from saying I was afraid to meet

	them and let them question me, and I want the Christian world to know that any atheist, agnostic, unbeliever, can question me anytime as to my belief in God, and I will answer him.
Darrow:	I want to take an exception to this conduct of this witness. He may be very popular down here in the hills. . . .
Bryan:	Your honor, they have not asked a question legally and the only reason they have asked any question is for the purpose, as the question about Jonah was asked, for a chance to give this agnostic an opportunity to criticize a believer in the world of God; and I answered the question in order to shut his mouth so that he cannot go out and tell his atheistic friends that I would not answer his questions. That is the only reason, no more reason in the world.
Malone:	Your honor on this very subject, I would like to say that I would have asked Mr. Bryan—and I consider myself as good a Christian as he is—every question that Mr. Darrow has asked him for the purpose of bring out whether or not there is to be taken in this court a literal interpretation of the Bible, or whether, obviously, as these questions indicate, if a general and literal construction cannot be put upon the parts of the Bible which have been covered by Mr. Darrow's questions. I hope for the last time no further attempt will be made by counsel on the other side of the case, or Mr. Bryan, to say the defense is concerned at all with Mr. Darrow's particular religious views or lack of religious views. We are here as lawyers with the same right to our views. I have the same right to mine as a Christian as Mr. Bryan has to his, and we do not intend to have this case charged by Mr. Darrow's agnosticism or Mr. Bryan's brand of Christianity. (A great applause.)

Mr. Darrow:

- **Q:** Mr. Bryan, do you believe that the first woman was Eve?
- **A:** Yes.
- **Q:** Do you believe she was literally made out of Adams's rib?
- **A:** I do.
- **Q:** Did you ever discover where Cain got his wife?
- **A:** No, sir; I leave the agnostics to hunt for her.
- **Q:** You have never found out?
- **A:** I have never tried to find
- **Q:** You have never tried to find?
- **A:** No.
- **Q:** The Bible says he got one, doesn't it? Were there other people on the earth at that time?
- **A:** I cannot say.
- **Q:** You cannot say. Did that ever enter your consideration?
- **A:** Never bothered me.

Q: There were no others recorded, but Cain got a wife.
A: That is what the Bible says.
Q: Where she came from you do not know. All right. Does the statement, "The morning and the evening were the first day," and "The morning and the evening were the second day," mean anything to you?
A: I do not think it necessarily means a twenty-four-hour day.
Q: You do not?
A: No.
Q: What do you consider it to be?
A: I have not attempted to explain it. If you will take the second chapter—let me have the book. (Examining Bible.) The fourth verse of the second chapter says: "These are the generations of the heavens and of the earth, when they were created in the day that the Lord God made the earth and the heavens," the word "day" there in the very next chapter is used to describe a period. I do not see that there is any necessity for construing the words, "the evening and the morning," as meaning necessarily a twenty-four-hour day, "in the day when the Lord made the heaven and the earth."
Q: Then, when the Bible said, for instance, "and God called the firmament heaven. And the evening and the morning were the second day," that does not necessarily mean twenty-four hours?
A: I do not think it necessarily does.
Q: Do you think it does or does not?
A: I know a great many think so.
Q: What do you think?
A: I do not think it does.
Q: You think those were not literal days?
A: I do not think they were twenty-four-hour days.
Q: What do you think about it?
A: That is my opinion—I do not know that my opinion is better on that subject than those who think it does.
Q: You do not think that?
A: No. But I think it would be just as easy for the kind of God we believe in to make the earth in six days as in six years or in 6,000,000 years or in 600,000,000 years. I do not think it important whether we believe one or the other.
Q: Do you think those were literal days?
A: My impression is they were periods, but I would not attempt to argue as against anybody who wanted to believe in literal days.
Q: I will read it to you from the Bible: " And the Lord God said unto the serpent, because thou hast done this, thou art cursed above all cattle, and above every beast of the field; upon thy belly shalt thou go and dust shalt thou eat all the days of thy life." Do you think that is why the serpent is compelled to crawl upon its belly?
A: I believe that.

Q: Have you any idea how the snake went before that time?
A: No, sir.
Q: Do you know whether he walked on his tail or not?
A: No, sir. I have no way to know. (Laughter in audience).
Q: Now, you refer to the cloud that was put in heaven after the flood, the rainbow. Do you believe in that?
A: Read it.
Q: All right, Mr. Bryan, I will read it for you.

Bryan: Your Honor, I think I can shorten this testimony. The only purpose Mr. Darrow has is to slur at the Bible, but I will answer his question. I will answer it all at once, and I have no objection in the world, I want the world to know that this man, who does not believe in a God, is trying to use a court in Tennessee—
Darrow: I object to that.
Bryan: (Continuing) to slur at it, and while it will require time, I am willing to take it.
Darrow: I object to your statement. I am exempting you on your fool ideas that no intelligent Christian on earth believes.
The Court: Court is adjourned until 9 o'clock tomorrow morning.

In the Court of Common Pleas of Lucas County, Ohio

State of Ohio,	)	CASE NOS. CR. 92–5256 and
	)	CR 92–6742
Plaintiff,	)	Hon. Franks
	)	
vs.	)	
Kenneth J. Barzacchini,	)	
XXKEM Corporation, and	)	
American Petroleum d/b/a/	)	
Lion Environmental Services, Inc.	)	
	)	
Defendants.	)	

Transcript of Proceedings

BE IT REMEMBERED, that on MOTIONS HEARING in the above-entitled cause, in the Court of Common Pleas of Lucas County, Ohio, in the September, 1992, term of said court, commencing on November 5, 1992, before the Honorable Ruth Ann Franks, one of the judges of said court, the following proceedings were had, to wit:

Appearances:

On behalf of the State of Ohio:

Robert Ashton, Asst. Attorney General, and Susan Ashbrook, Asst. Attorney General

On behalf of Defendant Kenneth J. Barzacchini:

Douglas A. Trant, Esq.

On behalf of Defendants XXKEM Corporation and American Petroleum d/b/a/ Lion Environmental, Inc.:

Susan Cairl, Esq.

On behalf of Defendant Nancy Walker:

Jill Hayes-Deckebach, Esq., and David Klucas, Esq.

Cross-Examination
By Mr. Trant:

Q: Mr. Kleinhenz, did you have a written sampling plan to go by when you went out to the site on the 21st or March 5th?
A: No, we don't have written sampling plans. We don't use them.
Q: You are familiar with SW846, are you not?
A: Sure.
Q: And that's—what is that?
A: That's the federal. U.S. EPA. Basically, it's our guidance document on sampling as well as sample analyses.
Q: And you know that they lay out very definite considerations and recommendations for a sampling plan?
A: On how to obtain samples; is that correct?
Q: Well, also a sampling plan of what you do before you ever get out there, don't they?
A: They might. I'd have to review that.
Q: You're not familiar with that?
A: Not that particular portion.
Q: One of the things that you're supposed to do is have an exclusion zone at the site, are you not?

MR. ASHTON: Objection, your Honor. If Mr. Trant is going to cross-examine the witness on SW846, I would request that a copy of it be provided to him so that he can–

MR. TRANT: Sure. If he wants it.

THE COURT: If you want to have him look at it. He says he's not familiar with it.
MR. ASHTON: I also object to the relevance.
MR. TRANT: Well, they went into all this on direct so–
THE COURT: Overruled.

By Mr. Trant:

Q: Were the jars that you had decontaminated before you took them out to the site?
A: Yes, our lab guarantees that.
Q: Your lab guarantees that. That's Chemtron that did that?
A: No.
Q: Who did it?
A: We get our sample, most of our sample containers from Chemtron.
Q: Chemtron. Well, did they do that? Did they decontaminate the jars?
A: Well, they—when they supply us the jars, they certify that the containers are clean. Each time we take samples we don't specifically ask them, are these containers that you supplied us clean.
Q: And you didn't do that in this case, did you?
A: No, we don't normally do that in any case.
Q: And, in fact, SW846 says that you ought to make sure jars are decontaminated so that you don't have contaminated jars that could skew or upset the sampling results, doesn't it?
A: I'd have to take a look at the SW846.
Q: Let me ask you this: All of the drums you sampled were not liquid, were they?
A: Many of them had labels on it. Again, I'd have to–
Q: Not labels, were not liquid, did not contain liquids.
A: Oh.
Q: Some of them contained sludge, for instance?
A: Correct.
Q: And you don't use a colowassa on sludge, do you?
A: It depends on the consistency of the sludge.
Q: Well, sludge is thick material, is it not?
A: It can vary.
Q: All right. Was any of this thick material?
A: I believe some of it was, sure.
Q: So, you didn't use a colowassa on that, did you?
A: Not on all the samples, no.
Q: Well, what did you use?
A: I'd have to refer to our sampling logs to let you know.
Q: Well—

THE COURT: Do you have those available?
MS ASHBROOK: May I approach the witness?

THE COURT:	Certainly.
MS ASHBROOK:	What I've handed the witness is the field log.
THE COURT:	Thank you.

Mr. Trant:

- **Q:** Can you answer the question now? Did you use another kind of sampling tool for the sludge?
- **A:** We used another sort of sampling device for—I haven't necessarily found a sludge, but mention of other sampling devices.
- **Q:** And what were they?
- **A:** Stainless steel spoon.
- **Q:** Now, again, SW846 for sludge recommends a trier, does it not?
- **A:** Probably actually recommends several different items.

MR. TRANT:	May I approach the witness, your Honor?
THE COURT:	Certainly.
MR. ASHTON:	May I see what you're going to ask him first?

By Mr. Trant:

- **Q:** First of all, do you recognize this collective document?
- **A:** Yes.
- **Q:** Okay. And that's SW846, is it not?
- **A:** I believe it is.
- **Q:** Okay. If you need to look at the other volumes of it to make sure, I'll be glad to show you but it–
- **A:** Okay, that's fine.

MR. ASHTON:	If I can enter an objection to the question? Apparently, the document is not complete based on counsel's comments.
THE COURT:	We're off the record for a moment. (A discussion was held off the record.)
MR. TRANT:	I'll just put it right here.
The Witness:	Okay.
THE COURT:	All right. We would note that counsel's provided a complete copy, what, is it all SW846?
MR. TRANT:	SW846, yes, ma'am.

By Mr. Trant:

- **Q:** Now, if you'll look at that and satisfy yourself of what that is.

MR. ASHTON:	Your Honor—

- **A:** Okay.

MR. ASHTON: —I'd like to renew my objection as to the relevancy of this. We're here on a pretty limited matter and—

THE COURT: Well, I think I understand where Mr. Trant is going, and I might be wrong; but the statement is—that counsel has made and then now made by the witness—that there is a very, very delicate procedure used to split the samples and you don't want to have them contaminated. And I guess what we're talking about now is the fact that procedures that are utilized in themselves are being challenged as not being specific in preventing contamination.

MR. ASHTON: Your Honor, there were no samples split here.

THE COURT: I know that. That's why we're here on this issue.

MR. ASHTON: I don't understand why what SW846 says about splitting is relevant. There were no samples split here.

THE COURT: It's talking about the way you should obtain the sample so it isn't contaminated, correct?

MR. TRANT: That's correct, your Honor.

MR. ASHTON: The sample in the first place?

THE COURT: Correct. And I think this is your argument, isn't it, that if they're taking a sample that's contaminated to begin with, their argument isn't supportive of failing to give it to the defendant because—

MR. ASHTON: Your Honor, this is something for trial. If defense want to—if the defendants want to attack the purity of our samples and the methodology we used in collecting our samples to attack our analytical reports, that's something for trial.

THE COURT: Well, we talk about the exculpatory value of the evidence. Now, is this exculpatory? Could it be contaminated? I don't know. Is that what we're going to?

MR. TRANT: Yes, your Honor, yes.

THE COURT: I mean, I'm just looking at the case law, and I think that it may well be becoming a real issue now. Overruled.

By Mr. Trant:

Q: Now you've had a chance to look at the whole document. Is that SW846?
A: Yes.
Q: And you're familiar with that?
A: Yes.
Q: That's the U.S. EPA publication which they supplement constantly. It's a loose-leaf publication, is it not?
A: I believe it is, yes.
Q: And one of the things they talk about is sampling in there?
A: That's correct.
Q: Okay. Now, the page I directed you to—

MR. TRANT: If I may approach the witness, your Honor please?
THE COURT: Certainly.

Q: Under this page, under "Drums and Sampling Tools," will you look at "Drums" and then find "Sludge" and see what the recommended sampling too is?
A: A trier.
Q: Okay. And what is that?
A: A sampling device typically made out of stainless steel that's used to take a core sample of a particular material.
Q: And that's so you get a representative sample of what's in the sludge; is that correct?
A: That's to take a column of waste through the sludge.
Q: Right. Because it's a long tube and you put it down and you draw up vertically a representative sample of what's throughout the drum and the sludge?
A: That's true.
Q: Whereas you used a spoon which just takes it off the top?
A: It can, depending on how–obviously, how far you go into the container.
Q: Okay. And who was in charge of rinsing those spoons from one drum to the other?
A: We used a separate spoon for each container.
Q: You used a separate 90 something spoons
A: Sure. Well, no, no, because each sample was not–each container that was sampled wasn't sampled with a spoon.
Q: And who is in charge of decontaminating the spoons before you took them to the site?
A: Well, the spoons that we use are new spoons that we get direct from the manufacturer, or from our supplier.
Q: And you didn't rinse them to make sure that you got metals off of them before you took them and got these samples?
A: No, these are brand new, clean.
Q: And don't you know that's recommended in SW846 as well that before you use these items at a site that you decontaminate them to make sure there's no contamination prior to using them?
A: Well, we're–we feel that the spoons that we use are clean.
Q: What about field duplicates? How many of those did you use?
A: We don't–we didn't take any field duplicates.
Q: You know that SW846 recommends that you take field duplicates don't you?
A: Well, I think it also depends on the types of samples that you're taking. When we take drum samples, we feel there's no need to take–as you called it, a field duplicate.
Q: Well, a field duplicate, explain to her Honor what that is.
A: Well, I'm not quite sure what particular definition that you might be using, but a duplicate sample would be a sample of the same material that—that you collected.

Q: And that's a quality control device, is it not?
A: Right.
Q: To ensure that your sampling results are accurate: is that a fair statement?
A: Well, it's—well, it's a quality control measure, yes
Q: And one of the things that SW846 talks about in developing a sampling plan is quality control. Is that a fair statement?
A: I'd have to review that section of SW846 but—
Q: Certainly, you would agree with that, though, that quality control is important in your sampling plan?
A: Oh, yeah.
Q: And that's one reason they recommend a sampling plan, and everyone that is taken out to the site to do sampling is supposed to be taught what that sampling plan is so everybody does their work consistently; is that correct?
A: And—yes.
Q: And that was not done in this case?
A: Well, we have—we don't have a written sampling plan that we have for each site. Our group takes numerous samples throughout the year, and we typically don't have the luxury of going out to a particular site beforehand to know what's out there in order to write a sampling plan.

So, we have an unwritten sampling plan. When we go out to a site there are specific things that we look for and those are the types of things that we'll earmark when we go on that site looking for, or going through the various waste streams that are all a particular site in order to sample them. So not knowing the specifics of each site before we go out there, we don't have a written plan.
Q: Well, you're supposed to have a person who is familiar with the site who can educate you as to what to look for, are you not?
A: It depends on the situation. Oftentimes when we go to a site, we're—we're the first people to go out there. So, there's no one that could give us that information.
Q: Well, you had Janet Liete Miller in this case, did you not, who was the—the inspector, Ohio EPA inspector—
A: Sure.
Q: —who had been out to the site numerous times?
A: And she could have stated that there were hundreds of drums on the facility.
Q: Well, she knew what kinds of wastes there were and so forth, and you had that information when you developed your health and safety plan, didn't you?
A: We had some information; that's correct.
Q: Well, you had some information as to what kind of matters to look for because you decided you needed to wear Level B protective equipment?
A: Right.
Q: But not everybody on site was wearing Level B protective equipment, were they?
A: What do you mean by "site"?

Q: On the pads.
A: Sometimes people were in Level C protection with respirators.
Q: And in blue jeans and regular boots?
A: Not the people from the EPA.
Q: Well, was there anybody on the pads that was doing—the subcontractors, were they doing that?
A: At times they probably were.
Q: And that can cause decontamination, can't it?
A: Can you repeat that?
Q: Well, for instance, if they track something up onto the pads and get it in the water, that—that can mean that there's something in the water that wasn't there before that person tracked it up there. That can decontaminate the water, can't it—or contaminate the water?
A: Well, there's various ways the water can become contaminated. That's certainly one way.
Q: But that's one, is it not?
A: Sure.
Q: And that's why you're supposed to have an exclusion zone that's very highly regulated, marked off, and nobody goes on it except personnel who have been taught what the sampling plan is and health and safety plan; isn't that right?
A: No.
Q: You're not supposed to have an exclusion zone?
A: No, that's not what I—
Q: Well, what are you telling me then?
A: Well, I answered your question and the answer to that was no.
Q: You're not supposed to have an exclusion zone?
A: That wasn't your question.
Q: Well, I'm asking you that now. Pardon me if I'm dumber than you, but—are you supposed to have an exclusion zone?
A: Yes.
Q: And the purpose of that is what?
A: Is–the purpose of an exclusion zone is to provide safety for the workers on site. You designate a certain area. Inside that area you're supposed to wear a certain level of protection. Outside that area you could wear a different level of protection.
Q: But isn't it also to make sure that you maintain quality control? Isn't that another purpose of the exclusion zone?
A: It's mainly for the health and safety of the workers.
Q: I know. You said that.
A: Right.
Q: But isn't it also to maintain quality control?
A: I'm not quite sure what you're getting at.
Q: Well, what I'm getting at is, if you have people that haven't been trained in the sampling plan, whatever it is, and the health and safety plan goes up on the pads, doesn't that affect your quality control?

A: Well, everybody that's on the pad wouldn't necessarily have to be familiar with the sampling plan if they're not going to be sampling. They need to be aware of what the health and safety plan is for their safety, but they don't necessarily have to be aware of what the sampling plan is if they're not going to be involved in that activity.

Q: They don't have to be aware of the sampling plan either?

A: Well, if they're not going to be involved in the sampling, there would not be a reason to.

Q: But, Mr. Kleinhenz, if one of the things you're sampling is this water that's on the pad itself, isn't it important for anybody that is just going to walk up on the pad to know what you're up there doing so they won't track something up there?

A: Well, yeah.

Q: But you didn't have that in this case, did you, quite frankly?

A: Have what?

Q: You didn't have a sampling plan that was taught to everybody who went up on those pads, including the subcontractors, to make sure they didn't contaminate the pad water?

A: We didn't have a written plan to inform them of that.

Q: Well, you didn't inform them orally, either, did you?

A: I don't remember.

Q: Who was your quality assurance representative on this project?

A: We don't have a designated quality assurance representative.

Q: SW846 under "Sampling Considerations" says that you should have one, don't they?

A: I'm not sure.

Q: Well, let me show you. Is that—is that what that says, Number 6?

A: Yes, it does.

Q: And does it say why you should?

A: Yes, it does.

Q: And why is that?

A: To help determine, or to document the accuracy and precision of the resulting database.

Q: Which is sort of real important, isn't it?

A: Yeah, yes, it is.

Q: But you didn't have such a person or such a plan in this case?

A: Well, we didn't have a designated person. I mean, our—the sampling that we do and the methods that we obtain our samples is correct. We don't have a problem with contaminating our samples. When we take a sample, we use correct methodology; and, in fact, that table you had showed me was examples that didn't necessarily state each and every type of container and the type of waste stream that you're sampling. It wasn't an exhaustive list of the types of sampling equipment. There's certainly other types of sampling equipment that you could use to take samples.

We feel that when we take our samples we take them correctly. The devices that we use are clean and not contaminated, so we could insure when it gets to the lab that's not going to be a problem with contamination.

Q: Did you decontaminate the colowassa before you went out there?

A: No, we use those one time and one time only, and those we get again direct from the—our—the supplier.

Q: And after you put these glass tubes down in the drums, what did you do with them?

A: I think in this particular instance, we saved them because our contractor was going to clean them and use them at his facility.

Q: In fact, you left them out on the pads didn't you?

A: I don't know. I know the plan was for him to take them away.

Q: So you don't know if he took them away or left them on the pads is your testimony?

A: Let's see, I believe he did at least put some of them in his truck. I can't testify to all of them.

Q: But certainly you're not testifying that a spoon is—is better at getting a representative sample of sludge than a trier which gets a vertical column, are you?

A: It kind of depends on how—how thick that sludge layer is. I mean, if it's a shallow sludge layer, then a spoon would be able to do the job easily as well.

Q: Let me show you this drawing, if I may, and ask you what that is.

A: That's an example of a sampler trier.

Q: Okay. And that's what we've been talking about?

A: That's correct.

MR. TRANT: Did your Honor want to see the picture here? It's this one here.
THE COURT: All right. Thank you very much.

By Mr. Trant:

Q: Now.

MR. ASHTON: May we see that, Mr. Trant, please?
MR. TRANT: Absolutely.
MR ASHTON: Thank you.

Q: —how many trip blanks did you take out to the site?

A: We didn't take any.

Q: Would you tell her Honor what a trip blank is?

A: A trip blank is, you would typically fill a container with distilled water, clean water and take it out to the facility that you're sampling at and then take it back and have that analyzed.

Q: And that's, again, a quality control device, is it not?

A: Yes, and it's primarily used and the reason why they use those, some of the samples that are taken are for wastes or environmental samples that may be of a low concentration of contaminants, so there is a possibility of—of contamination being involved and that's where it becomes really important. But in situations where your—the items or the waste that you're sampling are highly contaminated, the—that particular issue of having a trip blank isn't as important because you're dealing with such a highly concentrated waste or material that a little bit of contamination that would be—perhaps be detected would make a difference.

Q: Essentially, a trip blank helps you assure quality control in that it helps you take contamination or cross-contamination during handling or transportation?
A: Yes.
Q: And y'all didn't do that in this case?
A: No.
Q: Okay. How many field blanks did you take out there?
A: We didn't take any field blanks.
Q: And tell her Honor what a field blank is.
A: A field blank, actually, I'll have to probably refresh my memory.
Q: I'll be glad to show you this. If you could just read that to her Honor, and that's from SW846 again about a field blank.
A: Okay. "Field blanks should be collected at specified frequencies which will vary according to the probability of contamination or cross-contamination. Field blanks are often metal- and/or organic-free water aliquots that contact sampling equipment under field conditions and are analyzed to detect any contamination from sampling equipment, cross-contamination from previously collected samples, or contamination from conditions during sampling."
Q: So, what you do is, you have a system of filed blanks where you can take your spoon, for instance, and put it in this—in this device and it will pick up the contamination of the spoon; is that correct? Is that a fair summary?
A: Yes.
Q: Okay. And, again, that's quality control to make sure that your sampling results are accurate. Is that correct?
A: Right, especially when you're dealing with contamination of low level concentrations; but here we're dealing with wastes in the containers that are highly contaminated.
Q: Well, that's not true in every case, is it? For instance, you—you sampled a lot of drums that were well below the thresholds, EPA thresholds of hazardous waste, didn't you?
A: Well, not all their samples were—or I guess I'd have to take a look at the sample results to—
Q: In fact, most of the drums that you had analyzed, for every metal that was analyzed was well below the threshold of EPA toxicity; is that correct?
A: I'd have to review the sample results.
Q: Okay. That's the wrong notebook. Okay. Do you recognize that set of documents and what follows?
A: Yes.

Q: And a lot of that contains analysis of drums that were well below the thresholds of—of what the EPA has set up as toxic or hazardous?
A: At least for some of the samples; that's correct.
Q: And then some of the samples were just above the threshold, weren't they, for certain metals like lead, for instance, that kind of thing?
A: Well, what do you mean by "just above"? I just saw one that was 9.3 with regulatory cutoff is 5.
Q: Well, there's some with lead that's 5 and the sample shows 5.6. That would be just above, wouldn't it?
A: I haven't seen that one, but it's slightly elevated.
Q: Let me ask you this: There are numerous methods that are talked about in the SW846 as to looking for or sampling for metals, are there not?
A: Well, there are different metals so there is a technique for each metal. And there is also a total analysis as well as the one that determines whether something's considered a hazardous waste. Currently now it's called a toxicity characteristic leaching procedure, which is another method used to detect the amounts of metals in a particular sample.
Q: If you were going to test a drum for every possible hazardous waste metal that it could have, how many kinds of tests would you have to run?
A: Well, there's—well, all you'd have to state for that is you'd want the—if you can pardon the vernacular, you'd run the TC test for the eight metals.
Q: In fact, there are 44 such tests listed in the SW846, are there not?
A: For?
Q: For metals.
A: I've never counted them.
Q: If you would look at this page, and that—what is the—says—read that.
A: 33?
Q: Uh-huh.
A: "Methods for Determination of Metals."
Q: And read the methods available.
A: Pardon?
Q: Read the methods available with the numbers as to each one. Or you can count them, if you'd like; be quicker. Just count them.
A: Okay. Well, there's 26 on that page.
Q: Okay. Well, let's turn the page.
A: And there's a total of 43 they have listed there.
Q: Forty-three. Well, I miscounted then. And each one of those tests is expensive, isn't it?
A: I can't—I don't know how much these particular tests cost.
Q: But they're not cheap, are they, to get a lab to run them?

MR. ASHTON: Objection.

Q: Is—

THE COURT:	Is that an objection?
MR. ASHTON:	Yes, your Honor.
THE COURT:	Unless he knows the cost, I'm going to sustain it.

By Mr. Trant:

Q: And again, if I can direct your attention to another part of this, besides the testing for metals, there s several sample preparation methods that are talked about. are there not?

A: There are some, yes, uh-huh.

Q: How many of those are there?

A: Oh, five.

Q: And, again, that depends on what you're looking for, doesn't it?

A: That's true.

Q: Okay. And then there are—there are methods for looking for ignitability that are separate from those methods; is that correct?

A: There is a method for ignitability; that's correct.

Q: Okay. And also one for corrosivity or PH?

A: Right, but there's one—as far as metals, there's one test for hazardous wastes. I mean, there's other tests for various metals here that aren't a—wouldn't be considered a hazardous waste and there are different methods for those, but you're only interested in the eight metals that are for hazardous wastes. And there is a test method for that.

Q: There's only one test method?

A: There is an extraction procedure, and for each metal there would be a specific test to run once you ran through your extraction procedure.

Q: Well let me ask you this question, then.

MR. TRANT:	If I can have just a moment, if your Honor please?
THE COURT:	Certainly. Take your time.
MR. TRANT:	I'm ready, your Honor, whenever you are.
THE COURT:	All right.

By Mr. Trant:

Q: Mr. Kleinhenz, if there is only one method, why do you suppose the laboratory that y'all used, Chemtron, used some 15 or 16 different methods of testing on just the February 21st samples? And that wasn't the bulk of the samples. There were more samples in March, weren't there?

A: That is correct.

Q: Why do you suppose they used 15 or 16 different methods then?

A: For? There were—

Q: I'll ask you.

A: Okay.

Q: You check my math. How many methods did they list they used in testing those drums of y'all from the February search?
A: I believe there are about 16.
Q: And that's after y'all told them what to look for in each drum isn't it?
A: Thais correct.

MR. TRANT: That's all I have, your Honor.

A: But I guess, to clarify, I would like to add something to that. There were—

THE COURT: Do you have a problem with him continuing on?
MR. TRANT: No.

Q: Go ahead.

THE COURT: All right.

A: Listed in here were—we had requested samples for—to run EP toxic metals, which again are the eight metals to make it a hazardous waste. So, there's a leaching procedure for that, as well as a test method for the various metals.

There was also a request to run total metals as well, which is a different test. And typically, for each metal there would be a different test to run for that, and that's why there are several different test methods.

But initially, the question is asking about the hazardous waste end of it, and as far as the various test methods—or the types of analysis and what you have to request you would just again have to request to run the eight metals for the leaching procedure for, in this particular case, it was back when the EP toxic test was the test to check for characteristic.

Q: But they didn't use the TCLP, did they—
A: They used the EP that was what was needed back then.
Q: Which is now antiquated and doesn't accurately reflect, according to EPA, what's toxic or hazardous and what's not?
A: Well, they—they invented a new test which is now the TC test. Back then the EP test was the test used to determine whether a waste was characteristic or was considered a hazardous waste based on metals and a few other parameters. That was the test that was required.
Q: And the TC test was available then, wasn't it?
A: I'm not—it well, I'd have to check. It probably was. I don't know for sure.
Q: But your lab didn't run the more modern, more accepted test. They ran the old EP tox. test?
A: That's correct.
Q: Okay. And, again, there are how many methods now that they employed in testing these materials, twenty what, on the February drums? How many—

how many means of methodology were employed by your lab in testing these drums, the samples?
A: For determination if it was a hazardous waste?
Q: For their—for their results, how many are there? There are twenty something?
A: I believe I counted sixteen.
Q: Okay. And again, that's after y'all told them what you wanted them to look for?
A: Yes.
Q: Thank you.

MR. TRANT: That's all I have.
THE COURT: Redirect.
MR. ASHTON: Thank you, your Honor.

Clarence Darrow and William Jennings Bryan at the Scopes Trial

CHAPTER 3

CROSS-EXAMINATION BY PREPARATION

"Chase after the truth like hell and you'll free yourself, even though you never touch its coat-tails."

Clarence Darrow

The secret to any cross-examination is a thorough and exhausted preparation. Each known witness should be thoroughly investigated to determine what he presents for impeachment. Never take for granted that ones resume is accurate. Never take for granted that ones prior testimony was truthful. Never take for granted that a witness has never filed for bankruptcy, has no criminal record or other bad acts which may be used for impeachment. Always have your investigator talk to people who know the witnesses as well as thoroughly investigate their background. One can see the results of such preparation from Darrow's cross-examination of witnesses in the State of Michigan v. Ossian Sweet in which he successfully defended members of a professional black family who were charged with murder after shots were fired from their house into an angry, rioting white mob in racially tense Detroit.

Some of the areas which you may want to investigate are as follows:

1. Criminal convictions.
2. Criminal record not resulting in convictions which may be used as a prior bad act.

3. Specific instances of behavior which may be applicable either to prove a character trait or to impeach a witness.
4. Personnel files.
5. Civil service files.
6. Internal affairs files for law enforcement officers.
7. Bankruptcy fillings.
8. Other civil filings such as divorce and personal injury lawsuits where fraud or perjury might be present.
9. Previous speeches by the witness.
10. Previous writings by the witness.
11. The resume of the witness. Never assume that the person has been honest on their resume. Check out each claim on the resume.
12. Ex-spouses.
13. Coworkers.
14. Neighbors.
15. Tax liens.
16. Previous testimony.

Testimony of Eben Draper

Prosecution witness Eben Draper, a member of the Waterworks Improvement Association, was outside the Sweet home at the time of the shooting. He was cross-examined by Clarence Darrow.

Q: When was the club started?
A: A long time ago.
Q: When did you first hear that a colored family was moving into the neighborhood?
A: That was a long time ago, too.
Q: Did that have anything to do with your joining the club?
A: Possibly.
Q: Did it?
A: Yes.
Q: You joined the club to aid in keeping that a white district?
A: Yes.
Q: At the meeting in the school was any reference made to keeping the district free from colored people?
A: Yes.
Q: How many people were present at that meeting?
A: Seven hundred.

Testimony of Alfred Andrews

Alfred Andrews was cross-examined by Darrow concerning a pep talk delivered at the Waterworks Improvement Association meeting by a man from the Tireman

Improvement Association, the group believed to be responsible for driving a black man named Dr. Turner from his home on Spokane Avenue.

Q: Did he tell you about the riot trouble they had in his neighborhood?
A: Yes, he told us about a Negro named Dr. Turner who had bought a house on Spokane Avenue.
Q: Did he say his organization made Turner leave?
A: Yes. He said his organization wouldn't have Negroes in their neighborhood and they would cooperate with us in keeping them out of ours.
Q: Did the crowd applaud him?
A: Yes.
Q: Did you applaud?
A: Yes.
Q: You feel that way now?
A: Yes, I haven't changed.
Q: You know a colored person has certain rights?
A: Yes, I was in favor of keeping the Sweets out by legal means.
Q: Did the speaker talk of legal means?
A: No, he was a radical. I myself do not believe in violence.
Q: Did anybody in the audience of five hundred or more people protest against the speaker's advocacy of violence?
A: I don't know.

Testimony of Ray Dove

Dove, who lived directly across from the Sweet home, was cross-examined by Clarence Darrow.

[Dove testified that there were more women and children than men outside the Sweet home on the night of the shooting.]

Q: Did you make any estimate of the number of women and children in a crowd before?
A: No, I can't say that I have.
Q: As long as the question was asked by the State, you thought you were safe in answering it the way that you did?
A: No, not exactly.
Q: Was there a crowd?
A: No.
Q: Was there any disturbance?
A: No.
Q: Do you belong to any organization or club?
[No answer.]
Q: Have you any reason for not answering that question? . . .
Q: When did you hear that Dr. Sweet had bought the place?
A: Quite a while before he moved in I heard rumors from the neighbors.

Q: Quite a discussion?
A: Yes, I guess so.
Q: How long before you moved in?
A: Six weeks or two months.
Q: You heard it from all the neighbors?
A: Yes, two, three, or four of them.
Q: You discussed it with your wife?
A: Yes.
Q: You didn't want him there?
A: I am not prejudiced against them, but I don't believe in mixing whites and blacks.
Q: So you didn't want him there?
A: No, I guess not. . . .

Testimony of Inspector Norman Schuknecht

[Inspector Schuknecht was in charge of the police who were guarding Dr. Sweet's home. He testified that with him on the night of the shooting were eight patrolmen, a sergeant and a lieutenant.]

Q: There was no one there when you got there? The time of your arrival is about 7:30?
A: There were people on the street, but they were walking up and down and there was no congregating. . . .

[Schuknecht testified, "I told them [my officers] Dr. Sweet could live there if we had to take every man in the police station to see that he did."]

Q: Did you see anyone armed with clubs or other weapons?
A: Not any time.
Q: What happened at 8:15?
A: Suddenly a volley of shots was fired from the windows of Dr. Sweet's home.
Q: What could you see?
A: I saw flashes of guns.
Q: How many shots?
A: About fifteen or twenty.

Testimony of Dr. Ossian Sweet
Sweet was questioned by defense attorney Arthur Garfield Hays.

Q: What did you do when you got home on the evening of September 9th?
A: First thing I remember is my wife telling me about a phone conversation she had with Mrs. Butler, in which the latter told her of overhearing a conversation between the motorman of a street car and a woman passenger, to the effect that Negro family had moved into the neighborhood and they would be out before the next night.
Q: When did you first observe anything outside?
A: We were playing cards; it was about eight o'clock when something hit the roof of the house.

Q: What happened after that?
A: Somebody went to the window and then I heard the remark, "The people, the people."
Q: And then?
A: I ran out to the kitchen where my wife was. There were several lights burning. I turned them out and opened the door. I heard someone yell, "Go and raise hell in front, I'm going back. I was frightened, and after getting a gun, ran upstairs. Stones kept hitting our house intermittently. I threw myself on the bed and lay there a short while. Perhaps fifteen minutes, when a stone came through the window. Part of the glass hit me."
Q: What happened then?
A: Pandemonium—I guess that's the best way of describing it—broke loose. Everyone was running from room to room. There was a general uproar. Somebody yelled, "There's someone coming!" They said, "That's your brother." A car had pulled up to the curb. My brother and Mr. Davis got out. The mob yelled, "Here's niggers! Get them, get them!" As they rushed in, the mob surged forward fifteen or twenty feet. It looked like a human sea. Stones kept coming faster. I ran downstairs. Another window was smashed. Then one shot. Then eight or ten from upstairs; then it was all over. . . .
Q: State your mind at the time of the shooting.
A: When I opened the door and saw the mob, I realized I was facing the same mob that had hounded my people throughout its entire history. In my mind, I was pretty confident of what I was up against, with my back against the wall. I was filled with a peculiar fear, the kind no one could feel unless they had known the history of our race. I knew what mobs had done to my people before. Toms [objecting]: Is everything this man saw as a child justification for a crime 25 years later?

Sweet was cross-examined by Robert Toms.
[Toms asked Sweet why his testimony differed in several particulars from what he told police on the day of his arrest:]

A: I am under oath now. I was very excited then and afraid that what I said might be misinterpreted . . .
Q: You admit, of course, that Leon Breiner was killed by a bullet fired from your home?
A: No, I don't.

My cross-examination of the case agent in United States v. Mooneyham follows. This examination details how there is no substitute for good preparation. It also clearly illustrates how every possible angle of cross-examination should be investigated.[1]

---

[1] Thorough investigation and preparation for cross-examination is always a team effort. In this case the successful cross-examination could not have been done without the investigation of Brian Knopp, of Brian Lee Knopp-Investigator of Asheville, North Carolina, Nikki Pierce, of the Federal Defenders Services in Greeneville, Tennessee who represented the codefendant and Tim Moore, my co-counsel.

Special Agent Johnson testified during my cross-examination in a pretrial hearing that he had never been disciplined. Our investigation subsequent to that hearing and before the trial showed that he had been disciplined a number of times for dishonest and violent conduct. The devastating cross-examination of him at trial helped us to obtain a not guilty verdict on two of the counts and a hung jury on six more even though they found several ounces of cocaine immediately adjacent to our client's property and had him under surveillance going to and from that sight.

UNITED STATES DISTRICT COURT
EASTERN DISTRICT OF TENNESSEE
GREENEVILLE

UNITED STATES OF AMERICA,	.	DOCKET NO. CR-2–00–65
	.	
GOVERNMENT,	.	
	.	
VS.	.	
	.	GREENEVILLE, TN
SHERIDAN MCMAHAN AND	.	AUGUST 7, 2001
GEORGE MOONEYHAM,	.	9:30 A.M.
	.	VOLUME I
DEFENDANTS.	.	

TRANSCRIPT OF PROCEEDINGS
BEFORE THE HONORABLE THOMAS GRAY HULL
UNITED STATES DISTRICT JUDGE, AND A JURY

APPEARANCES:

FOR THE GOVERNMENT:	DAN R. SMITH, AUSA
FOR THE DEFENDANT MCMAHAN:	NIKKI PIERCE, ESQ. ANTHONY MARTINEZ, ESQ.

FOR THE DEFENDANT MOONEYHAM:	DOUGLAS TRANT, ESQ. TIM MOORE, ESQ.
COURT REPORTER:	KAREN J. CULBRETH RPR-RMR U.S. COURTHOUSE 101 SUMMER STREET, WEST GREENEVILLE, TN 37743

PROCEEDINGS RECORDED BY MECHANICAL STENOGRAPHY, TRANSCRIPT PRODUCED BY COMPUTER.

THE COURT: Okay
MR. TRANT: Thank you, Your Honor.

CROSS EXAMINATION

BY MR. TRANT:

Q: Mr. Johnson, let me ask you a simple straightforward question, if I may.
A. Yes, Sir.
Q: During your 28 years as an SBI agent, were you ever subject to any disciplinary action for any misconduct as an agent?
A: The only one that was, that I'm talking about misconduct, was ruled on the clothing from American, when American Airlines lost my clothing, is the only one that I know of any disciplinary, what you would call disciplinary action. I was demoted from a supervisor.
  There has been internals in which I was cleared of wrongdoing also.
Q: Then why would you on June 15th when I asked you that same question, did you lie to me?
A: I'm telling you, I honestly—You said something about days off. I have never been given any days off in employment. As a matter of fact, I never even recall taking a sick day. Plus—
Q: Mr. Johnson, this court reporter, do you know her, who took the hearing?.
A: I do not.
Q: Does she have something against you?

THE COURT: Sustained.
MR. SMITH: Argumentative, your Honor.

Q: Is there any reason she'd lie and put something false in this transcript?
A: No. I would like to see the entire thing because I believe there's something in there about days off.

Q: There's nothing about days off.
A: Well, you—

MR. SMITH: Now he's being argumentative, your Honor.

Q: Did I ask you, during that time were you subject to any disciplinary action for any misconduct as an agent?
A: In which you were given days off, is what I recall.
Q: Did I ask you that question?
A: Yes, sir.
Q: And your answer was, I've had internal investigations done, but—
A: And the judge stopped it, as I recall it at that point.
Q: You raised your right hand and lied under oath?
A: Sir, I have never lied under oath.
Q: What do you call this?
A: Look, I know what I said from the stand, sir.

THE COURT: Let's ask questions and not get argumentative, please.
MR. TRANT: Well, I'm trying to get him to answer the best I can, your Honor.
THE COURT: Well, you can do better than that.

Q: Now, you testified earlier that you never wrote anybody in the State Bureau of Investigation asking to see your investigative files; is that right?
A: No, sir.
Q: You never did?
A: You—They said asked to see an internal investigation.
Q: Did you ever send a memo to Director Brian Beatty on January 9th, 2001?
A: I asked to see my internal investigative files.
Q: Well, now what's the difference between that and what you were asked, did you ask to see your internal investigative files?
A: There's personnel file, there's internal investigation files; and I testified in here prior to leaving the SBI I asked to see any internal investigative files and was told, and personnel file, I believe, and was told I could not do it.
Q: Well, let me show you this letter, this memo that you wrote Director Beatty, and ask if you recognize it.
Thank you, Mr. Tipton.
A: Yes, sir, I do. This is where I asked to see my internal investigative files.
Q: And you received a response; did you not?
A: I'm not—to be honest with you, I don't remember that. I was told by the legal counsel—

THE COURT: Look at it, he's going to bring you something here.

A: —That I—that I could not.
Okay. Yes, sir, I received that.

Q: And what does that say?
A: That's what I'm saying, I went—well, let me—it just says, I am in receipt of your memorandum to me dated January 9th, 2000 requesting that you be allowed to review all internal investigative files that list you as a subject. Pursuant to the State Personnel Act, you're entitled to examine your own personnel file. Therefore, you're entitled to examine any information in a file concerning an internal investigation resulting in a disciplinary action. I was refused to see my—I was told I could not see my internal investigative file, even though he said I could, by the legal counsel, Mr. John Waters.
Q: So you're saying even though the Director of the State Bureau of Investigation told you you could see any of your files that you weren't allowed to?
A: Sir, shortly
Q: Is that your testimony?
A: Shortly thereafter—
Q: Answer my question, please, sir. Is that your testimony?
A: When I went up to Mr. Waters, I was told by the Internal Investigative Officer, Mr. Larry Smith, that you didn't—you couldn't have access to it. He told me I could see them in which I was, a disciplinary action was listed. There are some where there was no disciplinary action that I really wanted to see because I understand someone had made a couple wrong statements in there. I was refused to see those. I went to the legal counsel of the SBI, Mr. John Waters, asked him to see—I wanted to see all internal investigative files. He said, you can't see them.
Q: You were allowed to see these four that were sustained against you; weren't you?
A: No.
Q: Didn't you say, wait a minute, I've got a note–
A: I know what he said.
Q: Let me ask the questions, please, sir. Did you say, wait a minute, I've got a memo from the Director saying I can see these files?
A: No, sir, I did not.
Q: Well, he's over legal counsel; isn't he?
A: Well, he left shortly thereafter as Director too.
Q: He's somebody else that didn't like you?
A: No, sir. Mr. Beatty was a fine man, and I respected him, sir.
Q: So he wouldn't have any reason to make this up that you could see them; would he?
A: No, sir. He sent the memo back to me.
Q: How many other people in the SBI lied on you in these internal investigations?

MR. SMITH: Objection, your Honor. What is the relevance of these questions? We got three things that they can inquire into, and what the relevance of that–
MR. TRANT: That's what I'm sticking to is what's in these three investigations.
THE COURT: Ask him. What is your question?

Q: My question is in these three investigations that we can go into, what other SBI officers lied about you?

MR. SMITH: That was not his question, your Honor. If you want Ms. Culbreth to read it back. That was not his question.

THE COURT: That's the question he's asking now, and the other one wasn't answered, so answer the last question.

Q: Answer the question.
A: Repeat the question, please, sir.
Q: What other SBI officers lied about you in those three internal investigations which were sustained?
A: Which, all right, which three internal investigations are you referring to, sir?
Q: Okay. Well, let's start, if you don't mind, with the one where you filed the false claim in Louisiana
A: Sir, there wasn't no false claim.
Q: Well, the allegation was false pretenses; wasn't it?
A: Sir, no, the, I was—it was misconduct; that was what was the allegation, but it was found as misconduct because everything that I said happened. The only thing is the Bureau says that basically they bought my clothes and that they weren't my clothes to file a complaint with to American Airlines.
Q: If you'll look at that, please, sir.
A: My goodness.
Q: Is that the final action report in that internal investigation?
A: Yes, sir.
Q: And what does it say you are alleged to have done?
A: It says false pretense.
Q: And what does it say, that was sustained or not sustained?
A: Facts support the allegation of the complaint.
Q: And what does it say happened to you?
A: Demotion in grade.
Q: Because they concluded that you filed a false claim with American Airlines for clothing that you never even wore in Louisiana.
A: Sir, I did wear some of the clothes.
Q: Didn't the Commission conclude that?
A: Yes, sir. Some of the clothing I did wear in Louisiana
Q: Why were witnesses who was down there with you say you never did?
A: I don't know who the witnesses may be, I don't know; but I can tell you I wore some of the clothing.
Q: Who is Betsy Honeycutt?
A: Oh, gosh she was an educator with the North Carolina DARE Unit who was later terminated.
Q: Did she go to that meeting?
A: No, sir, she didn't go to that meeting. She was at that school.
Q: And did she say that you never wore that clothing?
A: I have no idea, sir. I never got an opportunity to see the internal investigative file. I don't know what anybody said.

Q: Susan Forest?
A: I know her; Uh-huh.
Q: She didn't like you either?
A: I don't—Susan and I always got along with each other.
Q: Why would she have told the internal investigators that you're a chronic liar?
A: I don't know that she told them, the investigators that.
Q: It's in the file.
A: I've never seen the file, sir.
Q: Lee Guthrie.
A: What about Lee Guthrie?
Q: You know him?
A: I sure do.
Q: You know why he would have told them you're a chronic liar?
A: I don't think Lee Guthrie said that.
Q: Well, it's in the file.
A: I'd like to see that, sir.
Q: Well, we're going to give you an opportunity to.
A: I'd like to see that.
Q: John Vaughn.
A: I had some problems with John as an employee.
Q: He said you're a chronic liar.
A: I'd have to see that.
Q: Agent Woody, you know him?
A: Agent who?
Q: Woody.
A: Do not know an Agent Woody.
Q: You know an Agent Doughty?
A: Doughty?
Q: Uh-huh.
A: Oh, do I ever.
Q: He doesn't like you either, I don't guess?
A: I don't know. I don't know, you know.
Q: What about Special Agent Moody?
A: What about him?
Q: Does he like you?
A: I don't think so.
Q: Do you know he stated in one of these investigations that it will take the SBI years in that district to recover from you?
A: Is that what he said??
Q: Yes, sir.
A: Well, I'm sorry, sir, I have always tried to do my job as straightforward as I could. The day I retired I would hope my badge would be just as shiny as it was the day I put it on, and to me that badge is still just as shiny as when I put it on, sir.

Q: Well, it wasn't shiny to a lot of these other agents; was it?
A: Have you ever heard of jealousy, sir?
Q: Jealousy, is that what inspired all this?
A: You can ask some of these other local officers coming in. I don't know.
Q: Do you know why Dr. Honeycutt would say that you were very sick and potentially dangerous?
A: Do what?
Q: Dr. Honeycutt would say in this file to Internal Investigations that you were very sick, potentially dangerous, paranoid and on the verge of physically acting out, now why would she say that about you?
A: Sir, I have no idea. Is it—
Q: And, in fact, when you were told—
A: They still allow me to carry a gun. They let me carry a gun for 30 years and I'm potentially dangerous?
Q: And when you were told in the internal investigation that these people said these things about you, your response was, and I quote, "This whole thing is horse shit."
A: Well, if that was said, it is.
Q: And that's what you said; isn't it?
A: Well, if it is, if that was said, it is, sir, my gosh.
Q: What about Assistant Director Smith?
A: What about—I mean, what are you asking of me, what do you want me—
Q: Did he not like you either?
A: I have no idea.
Q: Well, he's the one that found, sustained the action in this investigation where you exhibited unprofessional conduct for making untrue statements concerning another SBI agent.
A: Sir, the Director of the North Carolina State Bureau of Investigation sustained—I know what they show on paper, but he's the man that makes the call.
Q: Director Smith took your statement, Assistant Director Smith; didn't he?
A: Which, which investigation are you talking about?
Q: You know which investigation we're talking about, where you accused—you told other agent that you went to a birthday party and Special Agent Henegar was involved with drugs; didn't you?
A: No, sir; that's a lie.
Q: Well, that's what they concluded. They sustained that; didn't they?
A: No, they did not.
Q: Yes, they did.
A: No, sir, it was not sustained. It was sent back to the district; and I kept asking the supervisor what was going to happen to that internal investigation, what are the results of the finding. He said, I think it's a mix-up between you and Agent Moody, sir; and I'm not, you know, I'm not going to argue about it. I took a polygraph and was told that I did not fail, but Mr. Moody was not offered a polygraph.

Q: You took a polygraph?
A: I sure did.
Q: You took a polygraph, and it was inconclusive, wasn't it?
A: I was told I did not fail the polygraph.
Q: You were told it was inconclusive?
A: I have no idea.
Q: And you refused to take a second one; didn't you?
A: No, sir, I did not.
Q: And you started cussing them then; didn't you?
A: No, sir, I did not.

THE COURT: Now, let's bring the temperature gauge down just a little bit from the lawyer and the witness also, please.
THE WITNESS: Judge—
THE COURT: Just answer the questions—

A: No, sir.

THE COURT: —In the ordinary course and tone, and you ask them the same way, Mr. Trant.
MR. TRANT: Yes, sir. Thank you.
THE WITNESS: Thank you, your Honor.

Q: Let me ask you further about that. You told them in that investigation your wife didn't like Special Agent Henegar; didn't you?
A: My wife didn't, didn't like Special Agent Henegar. As a matter of fact, she, she didn't like any law enforcement officer woman. You know, she was just a jealous woman.
Q: And what about, who is Sutton?
A: Do what now?
Q: Sutton, S U T T O N.
A: Give me the full name.
Q: That's all I know. You made a statement, you said—
A: I know several Suttons. I know Trooper Tony Sutton—
Q: Well, maybe this will help you. You said you, your wife did not like Special Agent Henegar. You also stated that you had not, and pardon me, your honor, fucked Sutton. Now, who is that?
A: Do what? No, sir; no, sir.
Q: You didn't tell that?
A: No, sir.
Q: They just dreamed that up and put that in that report?
A: Yes, sir, somebody has.
Q: And that was Assistant Director Smith; is that correct?
A: I don't remember that. I'm saying I don't remember saying that to anybody, Smith or anybody, sir.

Q: And that report, that investigation was sustained, referred to your supervisor with action to be taken at the division level to insure that such an incident does not occur in the future; that's exactly what they did.
A: And Mr. Barnes, sir, told me that he thought it was a total misunderstanding. I said, well, if you don't–why don't you polygraph Mr. Moody. The statement was, he is in administration. I mean you can be an administrator and lie too.

MR. TRANT: Mr. Tipton.

Q: Let me show you that document and ask you if that's the final investigative report from that investigation?
A: I'm not sure. It's signed by Mr. Giles Coleman, so I assume it is.
Q: And it says, and I quote, does it not, what I just read to you?
A: If says, referred to the employee's supervisor. It does not say the facts were sustained, which means apparently I was telling the truth because the facts did not sustain untruthfulness; and that's what I—
Q: What does it say down in the right-hand corner?
A: It says right here, sir, it says, refer to employee's supervisor.
Q: And in the right-hand bottom corner, what does it say there?
A: It says, level, level 2. Insure that such incident does not occur in the future; but it's nothing, I—If I was shown untruthfulness, it would have showed facts. Sustained.
Q: The American Airlines incident, you were demoted. We've talked about that.
A: Yes, sir, I was.
Q: In another incident you were ordered to go into counseling?
A: No, sir. I was told that I needed to talk to someone about the situation.
Q: You were ordered to go into counseling until the counselor released you; were you not?
A: I don't think I was ordered to, no, sir. I was told that they felt like I needed to.

MR. TRANT: May I have a moment, your Honor?

Q: Well, let me let you look at it. Does it say that was sustained?
A: Yes, sir, it does; and I, I said it was.
Q: And it says—
A: But it says old consultation.
Q: And what does it say at the bottom?
A: He was advised or directed to attend counseling sessions. I can't make the rest of it out; and that's what I said, I was told that I needed to talk, you know, to a counselor about the problem.
Q: What it says is that he was directed to attend counseling sessions with Psychologist in Asheville that SBI would arrange for. He was to continue until Asheville doctor contacted Dr. Walker and advised the counseling need not be continued. Signed right below it?
A: James J. Coleman.

Q: So you were directed to go to counseling?
A: Well, that wasn't the way it was put to me, but I agreed to do it.
Q: Well, you got a copy of this, didn't you; and it had to do with a family member; didn't it?
A: Yes, sir.
Q: And you were given direct orders; weren't you?
A: Sure I was.
Q: You don't always do that?
A: Yes, sir, I try to.
Q: You were told by your director after the Louisiana DARE meeting not to go to any more DARE meetings; didn't you?
A: Sir, I talked to my supervisor and took vacation and went with my wife; and let me tell you, this is America, sir; and when I take vacation, and as long as I don't do anything to embarrass the State Bureau of Investigation, I don't see where they can, you know, should control where I go and what I do unless it's an embarrassment to them, sir.
Q: Had your director not told you, ordered you not to attend any more DARE meetings?
A: No, sir. He said, you are no longer over DARE in North Carolina. Don't want you to do anything in the state with the DARE; and I didn't do anything out there other than to go with my wife to see old friends that I had made in DARE all over this nation, sir.
Q: Why did that investigation find that you made derogatory remarks about the current SBI DARE supervisor?
A: I didn't make those. A GBI agent made them, sir.
Q: Why did they find that you made them? Did they lie about you in that?
A: No, sir. I'll be honest with you, I had a director that wanted me real bad, and I don't know why.
Q: One of the many people that rapped you, hum?
A: I didn't say many. I didn't know none of these others. I don't know.
Q: You said they were jealous a minute ago.
A: I said if they were—no comment.
Q: In the internal investigation you admitted lying when you told the director you would not be involved in DARE any more. You admitted that; didn't you?
A: No, sir, I did not.
Q: Why would that be in that file?
A: I haven't, I haven't had an opportunity to see the file, sir.
Q: Well, it's in there. That was sustained, wasn't it, that allegation that you were untruthful and insubordinate and went to a DARE meeting?
A: Yes, sir; yes, sir.
Q: In violation—
A: Yes, sir, after he—
Q: That was sustained?
A: After he told me not to mess with DARE and I didn't mess with DARE, I went with my wife on vacation to the meeting.

Q: If a person would lie once under oath, they're likely to lie again, aren't they, Mr. Johnson?
A: Sir, I haven't lied in this courtroom, or I haven't lied in those internal investigations. I, you know, all I can tell you, that's the best I can do.
Q: And when you did not truthfully answer my question in June about disciplinary action; that's not a lie?
A: Sir, you—and I'm—
Q: Please answer.
A: Ask that question again then.
Q: When you answered–
A: Oh, I tried to explain; and as I recall, the judge cut it off. I had had internal investigations. Either Mr. Smith stood up or the judge or somebody. Anyway, it—that question was cut off.
Q: Why is that not in the transcript, Mr. Johnson?
A: I don't know. I don't know.
Q: Sheridan McMahan told you that he had a source on Jonathan Creek?
A: Yes, sir.
Q: Where is that?
A: To be honest with you, I don't know; but I think it's near the Tennessee, not Tennessee Line, but back toward Maggie Valley or somewhere. I do not know where Jonathan Creek is, sir.
Q: Now, you said you conducted surveillance of Mr. McMahan going from North Carolina to Tennessee; didn't you?
A: Sir, I didn't do any surveillance. I testified that I met with him, give the money, met back with him and took the drugs.
Q: Was the surveillance not your—
A: The surveillance was run by the surveillance team, sir.
Q: Was it done at your direction?
A: No, sir, it was not at my direction; that's just a thing you do on undercover deals that's going across state lines and stuff.
Q: And you don't know that the highway that goes from I-40 to Maggie Valley is Jonathan Creek Road?
A: Sir, I do not. I was not—I've never been in that area that I can recall, never worked that area. Mine was further west.
Q: Did you know that he stopped on Jonathan Creek Road on the 5th?
A: He told me he did.
Q: Now, let's see—Yeah. Did you know that surveillance saw him stop at a trailer with a rebel flag at around 11:04?
A: I, I think it's in there, in the surveillance notes; but do I know that for a fact, no, sir, I do not.
Q: And surely you had some of your agents go to that trailer with the rebel flag and find out who lived there; didn't you?
A: I have no idea what they done, sir. I can only testify to what part I played in this investigation.

Q: You didn't go, you didn't have them go interview that guy or find out who it is to see if he was a cocaine dealer?
A: I have no idea what they did on that particular day.
Q: No idea if any determination was made if he bought the cocaine at that place on that day:?
A: I can only go by what he said.
Q: Well, sometimes drug dealers lie to you because they're trying to protect you from ever knowing about their source; don't they?
A: I'm sure they do.
Q: I'm sure they do; and he told you that his source in Tennessee lived in a house; didn't he?
A: Right off I-40.
Q: And, in fact, Mr. Mooneyham lives in a trailer, doesn't he, you know that?
A: I don't know what he lives in. I've never been there, sir.
Q: You've never looked at any of the pictures or anything?
A: No, I don't believe I have.
Q: He told you that he was going to go buy a car?
A: Yes, sir, he did.
Q: Do you know whether he went to Mr. Mooneyham's to buy a car?
A: I do not know.
Q: So as far as you know, he had a perfectly legitimate legal reason for going to Mr. Mooneyham's to buy a car?
A: I don't know. I don't know. You know, all I know is what the man told me; that he had a source in Newport; that's where he was going to get the cocaine. After the first buy, he went back supposedly to the same source and on the third deal was supposed to get it from the same source; that's all I can tell you, sir.
Q: But my question is you don't know whether or not he went to Mr. Mooneyham legally to buy a car; do you?
A: Sir, I can only testify to what I did in this investigation.
Q: Was the money that you bought this cocaine with marked money?
A: We ran, I think, some serial numbers.
Q: Where is it?
A: I'm trying to think. I don't know
Q: Never searched Mr. McMahan's house to try to find the marked money?
A: I'm not sure, TBI may have. I'm not sure.
Q: Well—
A: Because—
Q: Part of the money was North Carolina money?
A: Sure was, but they—I'm saying they may have our—what we did because the—well, let's see, they didn't give the money that day. The $12,000 was not given, it came back.
Q: Well, the money that you bought cocaine with before was marked money.
A: I'm not sure, sir.

Q: Well, wouldn't it make sense to mark it so that you could trace where it went to?
A: Well, you can't always trace.
Q: Well, you can trace it easier than if it's not marked; can't you?
A: Well, yes, sir.
Q: What were you doing with Graham County Sheriff Odum in this investigation?
A: Mr. Odum, parts of the Cherokee Indian Reservation lies in Graham County, part of it lies in Swain County, part of it lies in Jackson County; that's why he was there. Plus, he had a helicopter, and we had talked about using a helicopter. We had the plane up on the 11th; and if the plane had to come down to refuel, we were going to put the chopper up in the air; and you never know how long they may have taken. Then, again, on the 17th; but it was raining, we couldn't get the plane and we couldn't get the chopper; so that's why Graham County Sheriff was mainly involved in that thing because he had a helicopter there.
Q: So it's important for you to work with local law enforcement?
A: Yes, sir; that's—I try to work with local law enforcement.
Q: Is that why your sheriff in your own county refused to work with you?
A: My own county?
Q: Yes, sir, Sheriff Frye.
A: I've worked with him for many, many years. I worked with him many times before I left the Greensboro District.
Q: You know he refused to work with the SBI because you may come work a case?
A: No, sir; that's not the reason.
Q: And now you're running against him; aren't you?
A: No, Sir. You don't file until January. Do I plan to? There's a great possibility, yes, sir.
Q: So when you say you're unemployed, you're really running for sheriff against Sheriff Frye?
A: No, sir. I'm retired. I retired after 30 years of service.
Q: And Sheriff Frye is sick in the hospital; isn't he?
A: Sheriff Frye has cancer, yes, sir.
Q: And I guess he doesn't like you either; does he?
A: He's never told me he didn't like me, sir.
Q: Did Mr. McMahan ever tell you that he could get the cocaine over in North Carolina?
A: The only thing I remember is Jonathan's Creek.
Q: Did he say on one of the tapes, I'll get it over here, I can get it over here?
A: Yeah, he was talking about in Tennessee, I think.
Q: When you all were in North Carolina, he told you that; didn't he?
A: Yes, sir, I believe he did.
Q: Okay, and you all were always in North Carolina when you were in the car talking to him?
A: Yes, sir. I never was with Mr. McMahan in Tennessee.

Q: And on April 17th he said that he couldn't get the cocaine that day, and that he hadn't talked to his source, he talked to his source's boy; didn't he?
A: That's what he said on the tape.
Q: Who was that?
A: I have no idea, sir. I was not on that surveillance or—
Q: He told Agent Williams over here that, that he couldn't go into his driveway because his source was blacktopping his driveway; remember that?
A: No, sir, I don't.
Q: Do you know that Mr. Mooneyham's driveway has never been blacktopped?
A: I don't know anything about Mr. Mooneyham's place. I've testified that I only know what the defendant McMahan told me. The Tennessee people work the Tennessee side, sir.
Q: So you really don't know anything about Mr. Mooneyham in this case?
A: Only what he said to me when he was extradited back,
Q: And that time he was talking about Mr. McMahan; wasn't he?
A: I don't know. He said, when a man gets, sometimes when a man gets down and out, he does things he wouldn't normally do.
Q: And he was referring to Mr. McMahan because he didn't have any money and had to buy a car; isn't that right?
A: No, sir. He—Mr. Mooneyham made the statement to me. Mr. McMahan's name wasn't even mentioned.
Q: But you don't know who he was talking about, do you?
A: Well, assumed he was talking about himself because he sort of had his head down.
Q: I'm not asking you to assume anything. You don't know who he was talking about, do you?
A: Himself.
Q: Well—
A: That's who. You're asking me who I thought, himself, sir.
Q: On June 15th at this same hearing where you said you were never subject to disciplinary action, you said that you weren't sure who he was talking about, didn't you?
A: I was not in his mind. I can only tell you the statement he made, sir.
Q: Where in any of these tapes that you've played with Mr. McMahan does he ever mention the name George Mooneyham?
A: I don't know of any
Q: Ever mention the name George?
A: Not in the tapes, no, sir.

MR. TRANT: Just a moment, your honor, please
THE COURT: Okay
MR. TRANT: I believe that's all I have. Thank you.
THE COURT: Okay. Anything else?

Darrow with Leopold (L) and Loeb (R)

Chapter 4

Closing Argument–Plea for Life

"I may hate the sin but never the sinner."
Clarence Darrow

There is no closing argument a lawyer can give which is more important or more stressful than pleading for life. Clarence Darrow set the standards in his compelling argument to save the lives of Nathan Leopold and Dickie Lobe. Darrow took a daring chance in pleading the boys guilty so that he could have the judge for sentencing without the political pressure on the judge a guilty verdict from a jury would have wrought.

Note throughout his argument that he uses psychological themes, which was a new frontier at that time. He uses what we call mitigating circumstances today. He argues to the judge that their life may some day have meaning if they are spared. Darrow could do nothing to minimize the horrendous nature of the crime, little Bobby Franks had been kidnapped and brutally murdered. In such a closing argument the lawyer, as Darrow did, must acknowledge how bad the crime was but seek to focus attention on the mitigating circumstances. He turned around the fact that they were rich as a mitigating circumstance. He also turned around the fact that it was a crime really without a motive to argue his psychological theory. He uses recurring themes such as the cause of the crime throughout his argument. Recurring themes are an important part of any closing argument, particularly one in a death penalty case. He argued, as we do today, that the buck stops with the sentencer to make him realize that he is the arbiter of life and death in this situation.

Darrow did convince Judge Caverly to spare the lives of Leopold and Lobe. His decision and sentence follows Darrow's argument.

I had an equally daunting case in trying to persuade a jury to spare the life of John Henry Wallen in rural Claiborne County, Tennessee after he was convicted of shooting a highway patrol officer ten times with a 22 rifle as the trooper sat in his car reading a magazine. There was no denying how horrible the crime was or how outraged the community was. Like Darrow, however, in my closing argument I sought to shift focus away from the crime and on to the mitigating factors. The mitigating factors we presented were many and included everything that John did which was good in his life and everything bad that had happened to him. We also presented compelling testimony, and I argued what a horrible effect this event had on John's family. And, like Darrow, I argued for mercy.

Fortunately the jury spared John's life. That decision became even more important after we had the conviction overturned on appeal. The State of Tennessee, then, could not seek death on retrial. We reached a plea agreement wherein John was sentenced to 25 years.

The jurors told us after the trial that the most compelling parts of the closing argument and the reason that they spared John's life was because of his family and mercy.

CLOSING ARGUMENT BY CLARENCE DARROW

I know, Your Honor, that every atom of life in all this universe is bound up together. I know that a pebble cannot be thrown into the ocean without disturbing every drop of water in the sea. I know that every life is inextricably mixed and woven with every other life. I know that every influence, conscious and unconscious, acts and reacts on every living organism, and that no one can fix the blame. I know that all life is a series of infinite chances, which sometimes result one way and sometimes another. I have not the infinite wisdom that can fathom it, neither has any other human brain. But I do know that in back of it is a power that made it, that power alone can tell, and if there is no power, then it is an infinite chance, which man cannot solve.

Why should this boy's life be bound up with Frederick Nietzsche, who died thirty years ago, insane, in Germany? I don't know.

I only know it is.

They pull the dead boy into the back seat, and wrap him in a blanket, and this funeral car starts on its route.

If ever any death car went over the same route or the same kind of a route driven by sane people, I have never heard of it, and I fancy no one else has ever heard of it.

This car is driven for twenty miles. First down through thickly populated streets, where everyone knew the boys and their families, and had known them for years, till they come to The Midway Boulevard, and then take the main line of a street which is traveled more than any other street on the south side except in the loop, among automobiles that can scarcely go along on account of the number, straight down The Midway through the regular route of Jackson Park, Nathan Leopold driving this car, and Dick Loeb on the back seat, and the dead boy with him.

The slightest accident, the slightest misfortune, a bit of curiosity, an arrest for speeding, anything would bring destruction. They go down The Midway, through the park, meeting hundreds of machines, in sight of thousands of eyes, with this dead boy.

For what? For nothing! The mad acts of the fool in King Lear is the only thing I know of that compares with it. And yet doctors will swear that it is a sane act. They know better.

They go down a thickly populated street through South Chicago, and then for three miles take the longest street to go through this city; built solid with business buildings, filled with automobiles backed upon the street, with street cars on the track, with thousands of peering eyes; one boy driving and the other on the back seat, with the corpse of little Bobby Franks, the blood streaming from him, wetting everything in the car.

And yet they tell me that this is sanity; they tell me that the brains of these boys are not diseased. You need no experts, you need no X-rays; you need no study of the endocrines. Their conduct shows exactly what it was, and shows that this court has before him two young men who should be examined in a psychopathic hospital and treated kindly and with care. They get through South Chicago, and they take the regular automobile road down toward Hammond. There is the same situation; hundreds of machines; any accident might encompass their ruin. They stop at the forks of the road, and leave little Bobby Franks, soaked with blood, in the machine, and get their dinner, and eat it without an emotion or a qualm.

Your Honor, we do not need to believe in miracles; we need not resort to that in order to get blood. If it were any other case, there could not be a moment's hesitancy as to what to do.

I repeat, you may search the annals of crime, and you can find no parallel. It is utterly at variance with every motive and every act and every part of conduct that influences normal people in the commission of crime. There is not a sane thing in all of this from the beginning to the end. There was not a normal act in any of it, from its inception in a diseased brain, until today, when they sit here awaiting their doom.

"The motive was to get ten thousand dollars," say they.

These two boys, neither one of whom needed a cent, scions of wealthy people, killed this little inoffensive boy to get ten thousand dollars?

Did they need the money?

Why, at this very time, and a few months before, Dickie Loeb had a three thousand dollars checking account in the bank. Your Honor, I would be ashamed to talk about this except that in all apparent seriousness they are asking to kill these two boys on the strength of this flimsy foolishness.

At that time Richard Loeb had a three thousand dollar checking account in the bank. He had three Liberty Bonds; one of which was past due, and the interest on each of them had not been collected for three years. I said, had not been collected; not a penny's interest had been collected,—and the coupons were there for three years. And yet they would ask to hang him on the theory that he committed this murder because he needed money, and for money.

In addition to that we brought his father's private secretary here, who swears that whenever he asked for it, he got a check, without ever consulting the father. She had an open order to give him a check whenever he wanted it, and she had sent him a check in February, and he has lost it and had not cashed it. So he got another in March.

Your Honor, how far would this kind of an excuse go on the part of the defense? Anything is good enough to dump into a pot where the public are clamouring, and where the stage is set and where loud-voiced young attorneys are talking about the sanctity of the law, which means killing people; anything is enough to justify a demand for hanging.

How about Leopold?

Leopold was in regular receipt of one hundred and twenty-five dollars a month; he had an automobile; paid nothing for board and clothes, and expenses; he got money whenever he wanted it, and he had arranged to go to Europe and had bought his ticket and was going to leave about the time he was arrested in this case.

He passed his examination for the Harvard Law School, and was going to take a short trip to Europe before it was time for him to attend the fall term. His ticket had been bought, and his father was to give him three thousand dollars to make the trip.

In addition to that, these boys' families were extremely wealthy. The boys had been reared in luxury, they had never been denied anything; no want or desire left unsatisfied; no debts; no need of money; nothing.

And yet they murdered a little boy, against whom they had nothing in the world, without malice, without reason, to get five thousand dollars each. All right. All right, your Honor, if the court believes it, if anyone believes it, I can't help it.

That is what this case rests on. It could not stand up a minute without motive. Without it, it was the senseless act of immature and diseased children, as it was; a senseless act of children, wandering around in the dark and moved by some emotion, that we still perhaps have not the knowledge or the insight into life to thoroughly understand.

Before I would tie a noose around the neck of a boy I would try to call back into my mind the emotions of youth. I would try to remember what the world looked like to me when I was a child. I would try to remember how strong were these instinctive, persistent emotions that moved my life. I would try to remember how weak and inefficient was youth in the presence of the surging, controlling feelings of the child. One that honestly remembers and asks himself the question and tries to unlock the door that he thinks is closed, and calls back the boy, can understand the boy.

But, your Honor, that is not all there is to boyhood. Nature is strong and she is pitiless. She works in her own mysterious way, and we are her victims. We have not much to do with it ourselves. Nature takes this job in hand, and we play our parts. In the words of old Omar Khayyam, we are only

> "Impotent pieces in the game He plays upon this checkerboard of nights and days, Hither and thither moves, and checks, and slays, And one by one back in the closet lays."

What had this boy to do with it? He was not his own father; he was not his own mother; he was not his own grandparents. All of this was handed to him. He did not surround himself with governesses and wealth. He did not make himself. And yet he is to be compelled to pay.

There was a time in England, running down as late as the beginning of the last century, when judges used to convene court and call juries to try a horse, a dog, a pig, for crime. I have in my library a story of a judge and jury and lawyer's trying and convicting an old sow for lying down on her ten pigs and killing them.

What does it mean? Animals were tried. Do you mean to tell me that Dickie Loeb had any more to do with his making than any other product of heredity that is born upon the earth? . . .

Your Honor, I am almost ashamed to talk about it. I can hardly imagine that we are in the 20th century. And yet there are men who seriously say that for what Nature has done, for what life has done, for what training has done, you should hang these boys.

As a rule, lawyers are not scientists. They have learned the doctrine of hate and fear, and they think that there is only one way to make men good, and that is to put them in such terror that they do not dare to be bad. They act unmindful of history and science, and all the experience of the past.

Still, we are making some progress. Courts give attention to some things that they did not give attention to before.

Once in England they hanged children seven years of age; not necessarily hanged them, because hanging was never meant for punishment; it was meant for an exhibition. If somebody committed crime, he would be hanged by the head or the heels, it didn't matter much which, at the four cross roads, so that everybody could look at him until his bones were bare, and so that people would be good because they had seen the gruesome result of crime and hate.

Hanging was not necessarily meant for punishment. The culprit might be killed in any other way, and then hanged—yes. Hanging was an exhibition. They were hanged on the highest hill, and hanged at the cross-ways, and hanged in public places, so that all men could see. If there is any virtue in hanging, that was the logical way, because you cannot awe men into goodness unless they know about the hanging. We have not grown better than the ancients. We have grown more squeamish; we do not like to look at it; that is all. They hanged them at seven years; they hanged them again at eleven and fourteen.

We have raised the age of hanging. We have raised it by the humanity of courts, by the understanding of courts, by the progress in science which at last is reaching the law; and in ninety men hanged in Illinois from its beginning, not one single person under twenty-three was ever hanged upon a plea of guilty-not one. If your Honor should do this, you would violate every precedent that has been set in Illinois for almost a century. . . .

Your Honor, if in this court a boy of eighteen and a boy of nineteen should be hanged on a plea of guilty, in violation of every precedent of the past, in violation of the policy of the law to take care of the young, in violation of all the progress that has been made and of the humanity that has been shown in the case of the young; in violation of the law that places boys in reformatories instead of prisons,—if your Honor in violation of all that and in the face of all the past should stand here in Chicago alone to hang a boy on a plea of guilty, then we are turning our faces backward toward the barbarism which once possessed the world. If your Honor can hang a boy eighteen, some other judge can hang him at seventeen, or sixteen, or fourteen. Some day, if there is any such thing as progress in the world, if there is any spirit of humanity that is working in the hearts of men, some day men would look back upon this as a barbarous age which deliberately set itself in the way of progress, humanity and sympathy, and committed an unforgivable act.

I could say something about the death penalty that, for some mysterious reason, the state wants in this case. Why do they want it? To vindicate the law? Oh, no. The law can be vindicated without killing anyone else. It might shock the fine sensibilities of the state's counsel that this boy was put into a culvert and left after he was dead, but, your Honor, I can think of a scene that makes this pale into insignificance. I can think, and only think, your Honor, of taking two boys, one eighteen and the other nineteen, irresponsible, weak, diseased, penning them in a cell, checking off the days and the hours and the minutes, until they will be taken out and hanged. Wouldn't it be a glorious day for Chicago? Wouldn't it be a glorious triumph for the State's Attorney? Wouldn't it be a glorious triumph for justice in this land? Wouldn't it be a glorious illustration of Christianity and kindness and charity? I can picture them, wakened in the gray light of morning, furnished a suit of clothes by the state, led to the scaffold, their feet tied, black caps drawn over their heads, stood on a trap door, the hangman pressing a spring, so that it gives way under them; I can see them fall through space—and—stopped by the rope around their necks.

I do not know how much salvage there is in these two boys. I hate to say it in their presence, but what is there to look forward to? I do not know but what your Honor would be merciful if you tied a rope around their necks and let them die; merciful to them, but not merciful to civilization, and not merciful to those who would be left behind. To spend the balance of their days in prison is mighty little to look forward to, if anything. Is it anything? They may have the hope that as the years roll around they might be released. I do not know. I do not know. I will be honest with this court as I have tried to be from the beginning. I know that these boys are not fit to be at large. I believe they will not be until they pass through the next stage of life, at forty-five or fifty. Whether they will be then, I cannot tell. I am sure of this; that I will not be here to help them. So far as I am concerned, it is over.

I would not tell this court that I do not hope that some time, when life and age has changed their bodies, as it does, and has changed their emotions, as it does,—that they may once more return to life. I would be the last person on earth to close the door of hope to any human being that lives, and least of all to my clients. But what have they to look forward to? Nothing. And I think here of the stanzas of Housman:

> "Now hollow fires burn out to black,
> And lights are fluttering low:
> Square your shoulders, lift your pack
> And leave your friends and go.
> O never fear, lads, naught's to dread,
> Look not to left nor right:
> In all the endless road you tread
> There's nothing but the night."

I care not, your Honor, whether the march begins at the gallows or when the gates of Joliet close upon them, there is nothing but the night, and that is little for any human being to expect.

Now, your Honor, I have been practicing law a good deal longer than I should have, anyhow, for forty-five or forty-six years, and during a part of that time I have tried a good many criminal cases, always defending. It does not mean that I am better. It probably means that I am more squeamish than the other fellows. It means neither that I am better nor worse. It means the way I am made. I can not help it.

I have never yet tried a case where the state's attorney did not say that it was the most cold-blooded, inexcusable, premeditated case that ever occurred. If it was murder, there never was such a murder. If it was robbery, there never was such a robbery. If it was a conspiracy, it was the most terrible conspiracy that ever happened since the Star-Chamber passed into oblivion. If it was larceny, there never was such a larceny.

Now, I'm speaking moderately. All of them are the worst. Why? Well, it adds to the credit of the State's Attorney to be connected with a big case. That is one thing. They can say,—

"Well, I tried the most cold-blooded murder case that ever was tried, and I convicted them, and they are dead."

"I tried the worst forgery case that ever was tried, and I won that. I never did anything that was not big."

Lawyers are apt to say that.

I suppose it may have some effect with the court; I do not know. Anyway, those are the chances we take when we do our best to save life and reputation.

"Here, your clients have pleaded guilty to the most cold-blooded murder that ever took place in the history of the world. And how does a judge dare to refuse to hang by the neck until dead two cowardly ruffians who committed the coldest-blooded murder in the history of the world?"

That is a good talking point.

I want to give some attention to this cold-blooded murder, your Honor.

Was it a cold-blooded murder?

Was it the most terrible murder that ever happened in the State of Illinois?

Was it the most dastardly act in the annals of crime?

No.

This nurse was with [Loeb] all the time, except when he stole out at night, from two to fourteen years of age, and it is instructive to read her letter to show her attitude. It speaks volumes; tells exactly the relation between these two people. He, scheming and planning as healthy boys would do, to get out from under her restraint. She, putting before him the best books, which children generally do not want; and he, when she was not looking, reading detective stories, which he devoured story after story, in his young life. Of all of this there can be no question. What is the result? Every story he read was a story of crime. We have a statute in this state, passed only last year, if I recall it, which forbids minors reading stories of crime. Why? There is only one reason. Because the legislature in its wisdom felt that it would produce criminal tendencies in the boys who read them. The legislature of this state has given its opinion, and forbidden boys to read these books. He read them day after day. He never stopped. While he was passing through college at Ann Arbor he was still reading them. When he was a senior he read them, and almost nothing else.

Now, these facts are beyond dispute. He early developed the tendency to mix with crime, to be a detective; as a little boy shadowing people on the street; as a little child going out with his phantasy of being the head of a band of criminals and directing them on the street. How did this grow and develop in him? Let us see. It seems to me as natural as the day following the night. Every detective story is a story of a sleuth getting the best of it; trailing some unfortunate individual through devious ways until his victim is finally landed in jail or stands on the gallows. They all show how smart the detective is, and where the criminal himself falls down.

This boy early in his life conceived the idea that there could be a perfect crime, one that nobody could ever detect; that there could be one where the detective did not land his game; a perfect crime.

What do we know about childhood? The brain of the child is the home of dreams, of castles, of visions, of illusions and of delusions. In fact, there could be no childhood without delusions, for delusions are always more alluring than facts. Delusions, dreams and hallucinations are a part of the warp and woof of childhood. You know it and I know it. I remember, when I was a child, the men seemed as tall as the trees, the trees as tall as the mountains. I can remember very well when, as a little boy, I swam the deepest spot in the river for the first time. I swam breathlessly, and landed with as much sense of glory and triumph as Julius Caesar felt when he led his army across the Rubicon. I have been back since, and I can almost step across the same place, but it seemed an ocean then. And those men whom I thought were so wonderful were dead and left nothing behind. I had lived in a dream. I had never known the real world which I met, to my discomfort and despair, and that dispelled the illusion of my youth.

The whole life of childhood is a dream and an illusion, and whether they take one shape or another shape depends not upon the dreamy boy but on what surrounds him. As well might I have dreamed of burglars and wished to be one as to dream of policemen and wished to be one. Perhaps I was lucky, too, that I had no money. We have grown to think that the misfortune is in not having it. The great misfortune in this terrible case is the money. That has destroyed their lives. That has fostered these illusions. That has promoted this mad act. And, if your Honor shall doom them to die, it will be because they are the sons of the rich.

When [Dr. Krohn, prosecution psychiatrist] testified my mind carried me back to the time when I was a kid, which was some years ago, and we used to eat watermelons. I have seen little boys take a rind of watermelon and cover their whole faces with watermelon, eat it, devour it, and have the time of their lives, up to their ears in watermelon. And when I heard Dr. Krohn testify in this case, to take the blood of these two boys, I could see his mouth water with the joy it gave him, and he showed all the delight and pleasure of myself and my young companions when we ate watermelon. . . .

I can never imagine a real physician who cared for life or who thought of anything excepting cash, gloating over his testimony, as Dr. Krohn did in this case.

Kill them. Will that prevent other senseless boys or other vicious men or vicious women from killing?

No!

It will simply call upon every weak minded person to do as they have done. I know how easy it is to talk about mothers when you want to do something cruel. But I am thinking of the mothers, too. I know that any mother might be the mother of a little Bobby Franks, who left his home and went to his school, and who never came back. I know that any mother might be the mother of Richard Loeb and Nathan Leopold, just the same. The trouble is this, that if she is the mother of a Nathan Leopold or of a Richard Loeb, she has to ask herself the question,

> "How came my children to be what they are? From what ancestry did they get this strain? How far removed was the poison that destroyed their lives? Was I the bearer of the seed that brings them to death?"

Any mother might be the mother of any of them. But these two are the victims. I remember a little poem that gives the soliloquy of a boy about to be hanged, a soliloquy such as these boys might make:

> The night my father got me His mind was not on me; He did not plague his fancy To muse if I should be The son you see.
>
> The day my mother bore me She was a fool and glad, For all the pain I cost her, That she had borne the lad That borne she had.
>
> My father and my mother Out of the light they lie; The warrant would not find them, And here, 'tis only I Shall hang so high.

O let not man remember The soul that God forgot, But fetch the county sheriff And noose me in a knot, And I will rot.

And so the game is ended, That should not have begun. My father and my mother They had a likely son, And I have none.

No one knows what will be the fate of the child he gets or the child she bears; the fate of the child is the last thing they consider. This weary old world goes on, begetting, with birth and with living and with death; and all of it is blind from the beginning to the end. I do not know what it was that made these boys do this mad act, but I do know there is a reason for it. I know they did not beget themselves. I know that any one of an infinite number of causes reaching back to the beginning might be working out in these boys' minds, whom you are asked to hang in malice and in hatred and injustice, because someone in the past has sinned against them.

Now, your Honor, I have spoken about the war. I believed in it. I don't know whether I was crazy or not. Sometimes I think perhaps I was. I approved of it; I joined in the general cry of madness and despair. I urged men to fight. I was safe because I was too old to go. I was like the rest. What did they do? Right or wrong, justifiable or unjustifiable—which I need not discuss today—it changed the world. For four long years the civilized world was engaged in killing men. Christian against Christian, barbarians uniting with Christians to kill Christians; anything to kill. It was taught in every school, aye in the Sunday schools. The little children played at war. The toddling children on the street.

Do you suppose this world has ever been the same since then? How long, your Honor, will it take for the world to get back the humane emotions that were daily growing before the war? How long will it take the calloused hearts of men before the scars of hatred and cruelty shall be removed?

We read of killing one hundred thousand men in a day. We read about it and rejoiced in it—if it was the other fellows who were killed. We were fed on flesh and drank blood. Even down to the prattling babe. I need not tell your Honor this, because you know; I need not tell you how many upright, honorable young boys have come into this court charged with murder, some saved and some sent to their death, boys who fought in this war and learned to place a cheap value on human life. You know it and I know it. These boys were brought up in it. The tales of death were in their homes, their playgrounds, their schools; they were in the newspapers that they read; it was a part of the common frenzy—what was a life? It was nothing. It was the least sacred thing in existence and these boys were trained to this cruelty.

It will take fifty years to wipe it out of the human heart, if ever. I know this, that after the Civil War in 1865, crimes of this sort increased marvelously.

If we fail in this defense it will not be for lack of money. It will be on account of money. Money has been the most serious handicap that we have met. There are times when poverty is fortunate.

I insist, your Honor, that had this been the case of two boys of these defendants' age, unconnected with families supposed to have great wealth, there is not a State's Attorney in Illinois who would not have consented at once to a plea of guilty and a punishment in the penitentiary for life. Not one.

No lawyer could have justified any other attitude. No prosecution could have justified it.

We could have come into this court without evidence, without argument, and this court would have given to us what every judge in the City of Chicago has given to every boy in the City of Chicago since the first capital case was tried. We would have had no contest.

We are here with the lives of two boys imperiled, with the public aroused. For what?

Because, unfortunately, the parents have money. Nothing else.

Babe is somewhat older than Dick, and is a boy of remarkable mind—away beyond his years. He is a sort of freak in this direction, as in others; a boy without emotions, a boy obsessed of philosophy, a boy obsessed of learning, busy every minute of his life. He went through school quickly; he went to college young; he could learn faster than almost everybody else. His emotional life was lacking, as every alienist and witness in this case excepting Dr. Krohn has told you. He was just a half boy, an intellect, an intellectual machine going without balance and without a governor, seeking to find out everything there was in life intellectually; seeking to solve every philosophy, but using his intellect only. . . .

Babe took to philosophy. . . . He became enamoured of the philosophy of Nietzsche. Your Honor, I have read almost everything that Nietzsche ever wrote. He was a man of a wonderful intellect; the most original philosopher of the last century. A man who probably had made a deeper imprint on philosophy than any other man within a hundred years, whether right or wrong. More books have been written about him than probably all the rest of the philosophers in a hundred years. More college professors have talked about him. In a way he has reached more people, and still he has been a philosopher of what we might call the intellectual cult.

Nietzsche believed that some time the superman would be born, that evolution was working toward the superman. He wrote one book, "Beyond Good and Evil," which was a criticism of all moral codes as the world understands them; a treatise holding that the intelligent man is beyond good and evil; that the laws for good and the laws for evil do not apply to those who approach the superman.

At seventeen, at sixteen, at eighteen, while healthy boys were playing baseball or working on the farm, or doing odd jobs, he was reading Nietzsche, a boy who never should have seen it, at that early age. Babe was obsessed of it, and here are some of the things which Nietzsche taught: Become hard. To be obsessed by moral consideration presupposes a very low grade of intellect. We should substitute for morality the will to our own end, and consequently to the means to accomplish that. Nietzsche held a contemptuous, scornful attitude to all those things which the young are taught as important in life; a fixing of new values which are not the values by which any normal child has ever yet been reared—a philosophical dream, containing more or less truth, that was not meant by anyone to be applied to life. . . .

It was not a casual bit of philosophy with [Leopold]; it was his life. He believed in a superman. He and Dickie Loeb were the supermen. There might have been others, but they were two, and two chums. The ordinary commands of society were not for him. Many of us read this philosophy but know that it has no actual application to life; but not he. It became a part of his being. It was his philosophy. He lived it and practiced it; he thought it applied to him, and he could not have believed it excepting that it either caused a diseased mind or was the result of a diseased mind.

I suppose civilization will survive if your Honor hangs them. But it will be a terrible blow that you shall deal. Your Honor will be turning back over the long, long road we have traveled. You will be turning back from the protection of youth and infancy. Your Honor would be turning back from the treatment of children. Your Honor would be turning back to the barbarous days which Brother Marshall seems to love, when they burned people thirteen years of age.

And for what? Because the people are talking about it. Nothing else. It would not mean, your Honor, that your reason was convinced. It would mean in this land of ours, where talk is cheap, where newspapers are plenty, where the most immature expresses his opinion, and the more immature the stronger, that a court couldn't help feeling the great pressure of the public opinion which they say exists in this case.

Lawyers stand here by the day and read cases from the Dark Ages, where Judges have said that if a man had a grain of sense left and a child if he was barely out of his cradle, could be handled because he knew the difference between right and wrong. Death sentences for eighteen, seventeen, sixteen and fourteen years have been cited.

I have heard in the last six weeks nothing but the cry for blood.

I have heard from the office of the State's Attorney only ugly hate.

I have heard precedents quoted which would be a disgrace to a savage race.

I have seen a court urged almost to the point of threats to hang two boys, in the face of science, in the face of philosophy, in the face of humanity, in the face of experience, in the face of all the better and more humane thought of the age.

I have become obsessed with this deep feeling of hate and anger that has swept across this city and this land. I have been fighting it, battling with it, until it has fairly driven me mad, until I sometimes wonder whether every righteous human emotion has not gone down in the raging storm. I am not pleading so much for these boys as I am for the infinite number of others to follow, those who perhaps cannot be as well defended as these have been, those who may go down in the storm, and the tempest, without aid. It is of them I am thinking, and for them I am begging of this court not to turn backward toward the barbarous and cruel past.

The state itself in opening this case said that it was largely for experience and for a thrill, which it was. In the end the state switched it on to the foolish reason of getting cash.

Every fact in this case shows that cash had almost nothing to do with it, except as a factor in the perfect crime; and to commit the perfect crime there must be a kidnapping, and a kidnapping where they could get money, and that was all there was of it. Now, these are the two theories of this case, and I submit, your Honor, under the facts in this case, that there can be no question but that we are right.

What is this case?

This is a senseless, useless, purposeless, motiveless act of two boys. Now, let me see if I can prove it. There was not a particle of hate, there was not a grain of malice, there was no opportunity to be cruel except as death is cruel,—and death is cruel.

There was absolutely no purpose in it all, no reason in it all, and no motive in it all.

I have discussed somewhat in detail these two boys separately. Their coming together was the means of their undoing. Your Honor is familiar with the facts in reference to their association. They had a weird, almost impossible relationship. Leopold, with his obsession of the superman, had repeatedly said that Loeb was his idea of the superman. He had the attitude toward him that one has to his most devoted friend, or that a man has to a lover. Without the combination of these two, nothing of this sort probably could have happened. It is not necessary for us, your Honor, to rely upon words to prove the condition of these boys' minds, and to prove the effect of this strange and fatal relationship between these two boys.

It is mostly told in a letter which the state itself introduced in this case. . . .

They lived close together, only a few blocks from each other; saw each other every day; but Leopold wrote him this letter:

October 9, 1923.

Dear Dick:. . . .

Now, as to the third, last, and most important question. When you came to my home this afternoon I expected either to break friendship with you or attempt to kill you unless you told me why you acted as you did yesterday. . . .

Now, Dick, I am going to make a request to which I have perhaps no right, and yet which I dare to make also for "Auld Lang Syne." Will you, if not too inconvenient, let me know your answer (before I leave tomorrow) on the last count? This, to which I have no right, would greatly help my peace of mind in the next few days when it is most necessary to me. You can if you will merely call up my home before 12 noon and leave a message saying, "Dick says yes," if you wish our relations to continue as before, and "Dick says no," if not.

It is unnecessary to add that your decision will of course have no effect on my keeping to myself our confidences of the past, and that I regret the whole affair more than I can say.

Hoping not to have caused you too much trouble in reading this, I am (for the present), as ever

"Babe"

Now, I undertake to say that under any interpretation of this case, taking into account all the things your Honor knows, that have not been made public, or leaving them out, nobody can interpret that letter excepting on the theory of a diseased mind, and with it goes this strange document which was referred to in the letter.

"I, Nathan F. Leopold, Jr., being under no duress or compulsion, do hereby affirm and declare that on this, the 9th day of October, 1923, I for reasons of my own locked the door of the room in which I was with one Richard A. Loeb, with the intent of blocking his only feasible mode of egress, and that I further indicated my intention of applying physical force upon the person of the said Richard A. Loeb if necessary to carry out my design, to-wit, to block his only feasible "mode of egress."

There is nothing in this case, whether heard alone by the court or heard in public that can explain these documents, on the theory that the defendants were normal human beings.

Is Dickey Loeb to blame because out of the infinite forces that conspired to form him, the infinite forces that were at work producing him ages before he was born, that because out of these infinite combinations he was born with out it? If he is, then there should be a new definition for justice. Is he to blame for what he did not have and never had? Is he to blame that his machine is imperfect? Who is to blame? I do not know. I have never in my life been interested so much in fixing blame as I have in relieving people from blame. I am not wise enough to fix it. I know that somewhere in the past that entered into him something missed. It may be defective nerves. It may be a defective heart or liver. It may be defective endocrine glands. I know it is something. I know that nothing happens in this world without a cause.

I admit that I hate killing, and I hate it no matter how it is done,—whether you shoot a man through the heart, or cut his head off with an axe, or kill him with a chisel or tie a rope around his neck, I hate it. I always did. I always shall.

But there are degrees, and if I might be permitted to make my own rules I would say that if I were estimating what was the most cruel murder, I might first consider the sufferings of the victim.

Now, probably the State would not take that rule. They would say the one that had the most attention in the newspapers. In that way they have got me beaten at the start.

But I would say the first thing to consider is the degree of pain to the victim.

Poor little Bobby Franks suffered very little. There is no excuse for his killing. If to hang these two boys would bring him back to life, I would say let them go, and I believe their parents would say so, too. But:

> *The moving finger writes, and having writ,*
> *Moves on; nor all your piety nor wit*
> *Shall lure it back to cancel half a line,*
> *Nor all your tears wash out a word of it.*

Robert Franks is dead, and we cannot call him back to life. It was all over in fifteen minutes after he got into the car, and he probably never knew it or thought of it. That does not justify it. It is the last thing I would do. I am sorry for the poor boy. I am sorry for his parents. But, it is done.

Now, Your Honor, I shall discuss that more in detail a little later, and I only say it now because my friend Mr. Savage—did you pick him for his name or his ability or his learning?—because my friend Mr. Savage, in as cruel a speech as he knew how to make, said to this court that we plead guilty because we were afraid to do anything else.

Your Honor, that is true.

We have said to the public and to this court that neither the parents, nor the friends, nor the attorneys would want these boys released. That they are as they are. Unfortunate though it be, it is true, and those the closest to them know perfectly well that they should not be released, and that they should be permanently isolated from society. We have said it and we mean it. We are asking this court to save their lives, which is the last and the most that a judge can do.

We did plead guilty before your Honor because we were afraid to submit our cause to a jury. I would not for a moment deny to this court or to this community a realization of the serious danger we were in and how perplexed we were before we took this most unusual step.

I can tell your Honor why.

I have found that years and experience with life tempers one's emotions and makes him more understanding of his fellow man.

When my friend Savage is my age, or even yours, he will read his address to this court with horror.

I am aware that as one grows older he is less critical. He is not so sure. He is inclined to make some allowance for his fellow man. I am aware that a court has more experience, more judgment and more kindliness than a jury.

Your Honor, it may be hardly fair to the court, I am aware that I have helped to place a serious burden upon your shoulders. And at that, I have always meant to be your friend. But this was not an act of friendship.

I know perfectly well that where responsibility is divided by twelve, it is easy to say:

"Away with him".

But, your Honor, if these boys hang, you must do it. There can be no division of responsibility here. You can never explain that the rest overpowered you. It must be by your deliberate, cool, premeditated act, without a chance to shift responsibility.

And I want to say this, that the death of poor little Bobby Franks should not be in vain. Would it mean anything if on account of that death, these two boys were taken out and a rope tied around their necks and they died felons? Would that show that Bobby Franks had a purpose in his life and a purpose in his death? No, your Honor, the unfortunate and tragic death of this weak young lad should be something. It should mean an appeal to the fathers and the mothers, an appeal to the teachers, to the religious guides, to society at large. It should mean an appeal to all of them to appraise children, to understand the emotions that control them, to understand the ideas that possess them, to teach them to avoid the pitfalls of life. Society, too, should assume its share of the burdens of this case, and not make two more tragedies, but use this calamity as best it can to make life safer, to make childhood easier, and more secure, to do something to cure the cruelty, the hatred, the chance, and the wilfulness of life.

Mr. Crowe . . . deserves a great deal of credit for the industry, the research and the thoroughness that he and his staff have used in detecting this terrible crime.

He worked with intelligence and rapidity. If here and there he trampled on the edges of the Constitution, I am not going to talk about it here. If he did it, he is not the first one in that office and probably will not be the last who will do it, so let that go. A great many people in this world believe the end justifies the means. I don't know but that I do myself. And that is the reason I never want to take the side of the prosecution, because I might harm an individual. I am sure the State will live anyhow.

I know that every step in the progress of humanity has been met and opposed by prosecutors, and many times by courts. I know that when poaching and petty larceny was punishable by death in England, juries refused to convict. They were too humane to obey the law; and judges refused to sentence. I know that when the delusion of witchcraft was spreading over Europe, claiming its victims by the millions, many a judge so shaped his cases that no crime of witchcraft could be punished in his court. I know that these trials were stopped in America because juries would no longer convict. I know that every step in the progress of the world in reference to crime has come from the humane feelings of man. It has come from that deep well of sympathy, that in spite of all our training and all our conventions and all our teaching, still lives in the human breast. Without it there could be no human life on this weary old world.

Many may say now that they want to hang these boys; but I know that giving the people blood is something like giving them their dinner. When they get it they go to sleep. They may for the time being have an emotion, but they will bitterly regret it. And I undertake to say that if these two boys are sentenced to death, and are hanged, on that day there will be a pall settle over the people of this land that will be dark and deep, and at least cover every humane and intelligent person with its gloom. I wonder if it will do good. I wonder if it will help the children—and there is an infinite number like these. I marveled when I heard Mr. Savage talk. I do not criticize him. He is young and enthusiastic. But has he ever read anything? Has he ever thought? Was there ever any man who had studied science, who has read anything of criminology or philosophy,—was there ever any man who knew himself who could speak with the assurance with which he speaks?

I can hardly understand myself pleading to a court to visit mercy on two boys by shutting them into a prison for life.

For life! Where is the human heart that would not be satisfied by that?

Where is the man or woman who understands his own life and who has a particle of feeling that could ask for more? Any cry for more roots back to the hyena; it roots back to the hissing serpent; it roots back to the beast and the jungle. It is not part of man. . . . It is not part of all that promises any hope for the future and any justice for the present. And must I ask that these boys get mercy by spending the rest of their lives in prison, year following year, month following month, and day following day, with nothing to look forward to but hostile guards and stone walls? It ought not to be hard to get that much mercy in any court in the year 1924.

Now, I must say a word more and then I will leave this with you where I should have left it long ago. None of us are unmindful of the public; courts are not, and juries are not. We placed our fate in the hands of a trained court, thinking that he would be more mindful and considerate than a jury. I cannot say how people feel. I have stood here for three months as one might stand at the ocean trying to sweep back the tide. I hope the seas are subsiding and the wind is falling and I believe they are, but I wish to make no false pretense to this court. The easy thing and the popular thing to do is to hang my clients. I know it. Men and women who do not think will applaud. The cruel and the thoughtless will approve. It will be easy today; but in Chicago, and reaching out over the length and breadth of the land, more and more fathers and mothers, the humane, the kind and the hopeful, who are gaining an understanding and asking questions not only about these poor boys, but about their own,—these will join in no acclaim at the death of my clients. These would ask that the shedding of blood be stopped, and that the normal feelings of man resume their sway. And as the days and the months and the years go on, they will ask it more and more. But, your Honor, what they shall ask may not count. I know the easy way.

I know your Honor stands between the future and the past. I know the future is with me, and what I stand for here; not merely for the lives of these two unfortunate lads, but for all boys and all girls; for all of the young, and as far as possible, for all of the old. I am pleading for life, understanding, charity, kindness, and the infinite mercy that considers all. I am pleading that we overcome cruelty with kindness and hatred with love. I know the future is on my side. Your Honor stands between the past and the future. You may hang these boys; you may hang them by the neck until they are dead. But in doing it you will turn your face toward the past. In doing it you are making it harder for every other boy who in ignorance and darkness must grope his way through the mazes which only childhood knows. In doing it you will make it harder for unborn children. You may save them and make it easier for every child that some time may stand where these boys stand. You will make it easier for every human being with an aspiration and a vision and a hope and a fate. I am pleading for the future; I am pleading for a time when hatred and cruelty will not control the hearts of men. When we can learn by reason and judgement and understanding and faith that all life is worth saving, and that mercy is the highest attribute of man.

I feel that I should apologize for the length of time I have taken. This case may not be as important as I think it is, and I am sure I do not need to tell this court, or to tell my friends that I would fight just as hard for the poor as for the rich. If I should succeed in saving these boys' lives and do nothing for the progress of the law, I should feel sad, indeed. If I can succeed, my greatest reward and my greatest hope will be that I have done something for the tens of thousands of other boys, for the countless unfortunates who must tread the same road in blind childhood that these poor boys have trod,—that I have done something to help human understanding, to temper justice with mercy, to overcome hate with love. I was reading last night of the aspiration of the old Persian poet, Omar Khayyam. It appealed to me as the highest that I can vision. I wish it was in my heart, and I wish it was in the hearts of all:

> "So I be written in the Book of Love
> I do not care about that Book above.
> Erase my name or write it as you will,
> So I be written in the book of Love."

Judge Caverly's decision:

In view of the profound and unusual interest that this case has aroused not only in this community but in the entire country and even beyond its boundaries, the court feels it is his duty to state the reasons which have led him to the determination he has reached.

It is not an uncommon thing that pleas of guilty are entered in criminal cases, but almost without exception in the past such pleas have been the result of a virtual agreement between the defendants and the State's Attorney whereby in consideration of the plea the State's Attorney consents to recommend to the court a sentence deemed appropriate by him, and in the absence of special reasons to the contrary, it is the practice of the court to follow such recommendations.

In the present case the situation is a different one. A plea of guilty has been entered by the defense without a previous understanding with the prosecution and without any knowledge whatever on its part. Moreover, the plea of guilty did not in this particular case, as it usually does, render the task of the prosecution easier by substituting the admission of guilt for a possibly difficult and uncertain chain of proof. Here the State was in possession not only of the essential substantiating fact, but also of voluntary confessions on the part of the defendants. The plea of guilty, therefore, does not make a special case in favor of the defendant. Since both the cases—that, namely, of murder and that of kidnapping for ransom—were of a character which invested the court with discretion as to the extent of the punishment, it became his duty under the statute to examine witnesses as to the aggravation and mitigation of the defense. This duty has been fully met. By consent of counsel for the State and for the defendants, the testimony in the murder case has been accepted as equally applicable to the case of kidnapping for ransom. In addition, a prima facie case was made out for the kidnapping case as well. The testimony introduced, both by the prosecution and the defense, has been as detailed and elaborate as though the case had been tried before a jury. It has been given the widest publicity and the public is so fully familiar with all its phases that it would serve no useful purpose to restate or analyze the evidence. By pleading guilty, the defendants have admitted legal responsibility for their acts; the testimony has satisfied the court that the case is not one in which it would have been possible to set up successfully the defense of insanity as insanity is defined and understood by the established law of this state for the purpose of the administration of criminal justice.

The court, however, feels impelled to dwell briefly on the mass of data produced as to the physical, mental, and moral condition of the two defendants. They have been shown in essential respects to be abnormal; had they been normal they would not have committed the crime. It is beyond the province of this court, as it is beyond the capacity of humankind in its present state of development to predicate ultimate responsibility for human acts.

At the same time, the court is willing to recognize that the careful analysis made of the life history of the defendants and of their present mental, emotional and ethical condition has been of extreme interest and is a valuable contribution to criminology. And yet the court feels strongly that similar analyses made of other persons accused of crime will probably reveal similar or different abnormalities. The value of such tests seems to lie in their applicability to crime and criminals in general.

Since they concern the broad question of human responsibility and legal punishment and are in no wise peculiar to the individual defendants, they may be deserving of legislative but not judicial consideration. For this reason the court is satisfied that his judgment in the present case cannot be affected thereby. The testimony in this case reveals a crime of singular atrocity. It is, in a sense, inexplicable, but is not thereby tendered less inhuman or repulsive. It was deliberately planned and prepared for during a considerable period of time. It was executed with every feature of callousness and cruelty. And here the court will say, not for the purpose of extenuating guilty, but merely with the object of dispelling a misapprehension that appears to have found lodgment in the public mind, that he is convinced by conclusive evidence that there was no abuse offered to the body of the victim. But it did not need that element to make the crime abhorrent to every instinct of human ability, and the court is satisfied that neither in the act itself, nor in its motives or lack of motives, or in the antecedents of the offenders, can he find any mitigating circumstances. For the crime of murder and of kidnapping for ransom the law prescribes different punishments in the alternatives. For the crime of murder the statute declares: "Whoever is guilty of murder shall suffer the punishment of death or imprisonment in the penitentiary for his natural life or for a term not less than fourteen years. If the accused is found guilty by a jury they shall fix the punishment by their verdict; upon a plea of guilty, the punishment shall be fixed by the court." For the crime of kidnapping for ransom, the statute reads: "Whoever is guilty of kidnapping for ransom shall suffer death or be punished by imprisonment in the penitentiary for life, or for any term not less than five years. "Under the pleas of guilty, the duty of determining the punishment devolves upon the court, and the law indicates no rule or policy for the guidance of his discretion. In reaching his decision the court would have welcomed the counsel and support of others. In some states the legislature, in its wisdom, has provided for a bench of three judges to determine the penalty in cases such as this. Nevertheless, the court is willing to meet his responsibilities. It would have been the task of least resistance to impose the extreme penalty of the law. In choosing imprisonment instead of death, the court is moved chiefly by the consideration of the age of the defendants, boys of eighteen and nineteen years.

It is not for the court to say that he will not, in any case, enforce capital punishment as an alternative, but the court believes it is within his province to decline to impose the sentence of death on persons who are not of full age.

This determination appears to be in accordance with the progress of criminal law all over the world and with the dictates of enlightened humanity. More than that, it seems to be in accordance with the precedents hereto observed in this State. The records of Illinois show only two cases of minors who were put to death by legal process . . . to which number the court does not feel inclined to make an addition.

Life imprisonment, at the moment, strikes the public imagination as forcibly as would death by hanging, but to the offenders, particularly of the type they are, the prolonged suffering of years of confinement may well be the severest form of retribution and expiation.

The court feels it proper to add a final word concerning the effect of the parole law upon the punishment of these defendants. In the case of such atrocious crimes, it is entirely within the discretion of the department of public welfare, never to admit these defendants to parole.

To such a policy the court urges them strictly to adhere; if this course is persevered in the punishment of these defendants, it will both satisfy the ends of justice and safeguard the interests of society.

[At this point the sentences formally were passed as follows:]
"In no. 33,623, indictment for murder, the sentence of the court is that you, Nathan F. Leopold, Jr., be confined in the penitentiary at Joliet for the term of your natural life. The court finds that your age is 19.

"In no. 33,623, indictment for murder, the sentence of the court is that you, Richard Loeb, be confined in the penitentiary at Joliet for the term of your natural life. The court finds that your age is 18.

"In 33,624, kidnapping for ransom, it is the sentence of the court that you, Nathan F. Leopold, Jr. be confined in the penitentiary at Joliet for the term of 99 years. The court finds your age at 19.

"In 33,624, kidnapping for ransom, the sentence of the court is that you, Richard Loeb, be confined in the penitentiary at Joliet for the term of 99 years."

CLOSING ARGUMENT BY DOUGLAS A. TRANT ON BEHALF OF THE DEFENDANT JOHN HENRY WALLEN

Thank you very much, Your Honor.

Ladies and gentlemen, we are not talking about getting out of anything, about no punishment. If you give John Wallen a life sentence, that will be his punishment. Because he will serve the rest of his life in the State penitentiary. That is a severe penalty for anybody. There is no question about that. But there is no point in compounding the suffering in this case. Look at these folks back here. You have seen them testify, you have seen their hurt, you have seen them beg you not to kill their boy. And that is clearly in your hands. All they ask is, put him in the penitentiary for the rest of his life, we can go visit him on visiting days, he can work and be productive in the penitentiary, but please, I beg you, don't kill him.

That is not only the merciful thing do to in this case, but I submit to you that it is the just thing to do, and the right thing to do.

In this part of the case you haven't heard anything new from the prosecutors. You heard it all in the guilty phase. And they have only alleged one aggravating circumstance.

In the statute it is written where there are other possible aggravating circumstances, like if somebody has a violent felony record. Or they killed more than one person. Or they do it in the course of a robbery or something like that. Those are the kinds of people I submit to you that the Legislature had most in mind when they wrote the statute. But you have only heard one circumstance, one aggravating circumstance about John Wallen.

We are not seeking to minimize the loss to the Tripp family. But, we are asking you to punish him for that for the rest of his life, that he wakes up everyday in the penitentiary. Don't punish his dad, his mama, his sisters, his brothers. You heard Vickie Braden, it will kill her folks. And you shouldn't do it. The decision is in your hands. And you shouldn't do it. You shouldn't do it. I submit to you, because this one aggravating circumstances does not outweigh the mitigating. The Judge is going to instruct you that you should consider all of things, and you can't refuse to consider all of this mitigation.

You have heard the teachers talk about–Lynn Barnard, Billy Myers, Ed Howerton, Billie King, Dillon Shockley, all of them testified consistently that–yeah, John may have been below average in some of his studies, yeah, he had trouble with figures and so forth, but he was a good kid, he was a well behaved kid, he tried, he put his best foot forward. And that is what he did. And that ought to count for something in life. No matter what you have done, it ought to count for something and that is why the Judge is going to tell you you can consider those things, because it counts for something. And you ought to consider that. It is important.

The good that you do in life ought to speak for you. And it does. And that is why you, as jurors, should consider it.

You heard Ben Jolly, he testified that John did a good job driving the ambulance. And I submit to you ladies and gentlemen, that there are people who wouldn't be with us today, alive, if John Wallen hadn't done a good job driving that ambulance. That he helped save lives. And that ought to count for something.

And then you heard two individuals come in here and tell you how he helped them. Danny Hubbard. Who knows what would have happened to Danny Hubbard if John hadn't been able to get him out of that car, or get the car off his head? Take him a long distance in the night to his folks so that he could get help. Danny might not be able to come here and talk to y'all today. That is a life that is here because of John Wallen. And that ought to count for something. He ought to get credit for doing that. And that is what considering that is all about.

Elmer Posey, I can only imagine how bad his legs must have been busted up with a bulldozer running over him, and falling over. He had to be hurt badly. Probably going into shock. And it was because John Wallen came and helped him in a very professional way that maybe is the reason he has still got his legs. And that ought to count for something. The good deed John did that day. He could have been doing something else. But he was doing that and he did it well, he did it effectively, and he ought to get credit for that.

Wayne Rowlette, supervisor at Lance. John did a good job. Rick Brooks told you how he did a good job. He needed help, and Rich had to help him with the paperwork, because John has a hard time with that. And you have seen, no matter who you believe with the psychologist, he has a hard time with verbal things, with communication things. Even with the State's own psychologist, falling below the floor in communication skills. The lowest percentile ranking he can be in. But he needed help with it, and John's history is, when he was in school, when he was with the ambulance service, when he worked for Lance, that he tried hard, he worked extra hours, he put his best foot forward. And it is common sense. We ought to get credit for that in life. And you, ladies and gentlemen of the jury, ought to give him credit for doing that.

Yvonne Ellison, and I add to this down here, as I failed to put it in, a good neighbor. She testified that she would be proud to have John as a son. Because he helped her. He helped her fix the lawnmower, he helped, you know, get the tobacco in, and get it up. Helped her with her dad, taking him to the hospital. That is a good deed. He didn't have to do that. And he ought to get credit for doing it. That is the way we work in our society. Get credit for your good deeds.

Roman Sharp. Stipulated testimony, Roman Sharp says that he is a guard at the Knox County Jail, and the year that John has been held, awaiting this trial, and that he was a good prisoner, followed instructions, didn't cause trouble, never tried to escape, and if he has done it for the last year, you can assume he will do it for the rest of his life. He is not a danger to escape. He is not a danger to cause trouble, he had proved in over the last year. You can trust him to go to the penitentiary and behave himself and be productive. He has always wanted to work. And there are work programs within the walls of the penitentiary that benefit us in society. Benefit us greatly. And he is the kind of person that can do that. And be of benefit to all of us, and his folks know that he is there.

Whatever it was that caused the pain that he is experiencing, that everybody is experiencing, and that his family experiences, it doesn't get any better by strapping him in the electric chair. We know that. We know that. And we know that there is a punishment that you can give him, that is a stern punishment, where he is never out in society again. And that is to put him in the penitentiary for the rest of his life.

One aggravating circumstance clearly does not outweigh the twenty-one mitigating circumstances that have been proven to you and that Judge will instruct you, as a matter of law, to consider. One, John has been a good son to his parents. No question about that. They have told you about that. He ought to get credit for that. Some kids aren't good kids to their parents. The people that are ought to get credit for it in our society. And John ought to get credit for it.

John has been a good brother. No question about that. His brothers and sisters are here, they have told you that, he ought to get credit for that.

He was a well behaved student, put his best foot forward. Again, no question about that. The evidence clearly shows that. His teachers told you that. That he was a well disciplined kid. And that he tried, they liked him, and he did put his best foot forward, even though he had some deficiencies.

He was a good ambulance driver and helped save numerous lives. No question about that. That is true from the proof. And he ought to get credit for that.

He was very skilled with the Jaws of Life and helped free people who were trapped in cars. You can imagine what it is like to be trapped in a car. I hope none of you ever have. But if you are, you want somebody like John Wallen to come get you out so you can get help, get free. And he has done that and he has helped people. He ought to get credit for that.

That the hospital never had any complaints about John when he worked with the ambulance service. That shows that he was consistent in good work, consistently helped people and he ought to get credit for that.

He did a good job for Lance. He was honest and hard working. Everybody was in agreement with that. It was absolutely true. And people who are honest and hard working, whatever kind of job is involved, ought to get credit for doing that.

His customers found him efficient. Absolutely true. Nobody complained to Rick Brooks after John left. And he ought to get credit for serving his customers the way that he did.

That he put in extra hours for Lance, with help from his girlfriend, Sandra, and Rick Brooks to get his paperwork done. He wanted to do his job right. And he was willing to work a lot of extra hours. And how many people in society today are willing to do that? You know, when the time clock goes off, they are gone. He wanted to put in extra hours to do his job right. And he enlisted help to do that. He ought to get credit for doing that.

He has been a good prisoner, no question about that. No proof to the contrary. And the proof is that he has, he has followed instructions, and he has not tried to escape. He has behaved himself, and he ought to get credit for that record.

That he rehabilitated himself after a serious automobile accident in '87, in the hospital for six weeks. Legs crushed. But he fought his way back and went back to work and became productive again. And he ought to get credit for doing that.

That he has been a productive worker, even though he needs help with his daily living skills. He has a hard time with some of his daily living skills. Sandra Arnold told you that. He can't fix a box of macaroni and cheese with a recipe, he doesn't know how to do a load of laundry. And he ought to get some credit for trying, even when he messed it up, and for getting out and being productive in society, even though he didn't have the same skills as you and I, that he was disadvantaged. And there is no question but that he was.

John was not able to graduate from high school but had to get a Certificate of Attendance because he couldn't pass the Tennessee Proficiency Test. Think about that for a moment. Designed for sixth to eighth grade level and the only one he could ever pass was the one that he was put in a special class for, the VIP math class, which taught the test. And he took the test four times. Over and over again. Just like he took the EMT test over and over and over again. He was trying. But he couldn't do it. He just didn't have the mental ability to do it, but he ought to be given credit for the fact that he tried.

That John is mentally retarded, does not possess the ability of normal people to get along in life. And I submit to you that the proof shows that. Dr. McCoy spent hours with him and gave him tests that are recognized by anyone in psychology as being valid tests. And the test results were consistently in the mentally retarded range.

And even when Dr. Allen gave him the test, the test scores were consistently in the mentally retarded range. Some of them in the lower bottom, where they couldn't even score. And Dr. Allen has stated for you, well, I can't say yes, I can't say not–well, that is a wash. But Dr. McCoy says that she believes that he is from the test scores that he got, from talking to people that he knows, about his difficulty in getting along in a daily fashion. And by his proficiency scores. And remember, she said that someone who is mildly mentally retarded can do a lot of things in life. Can be productive. They have a hard time with communication skills, the verbal things, but if they are taught things over and over again, a lot of times they can pick them up and they can perform service jobs. And that is what he did with a lot of effort, but he did it, he tried, he put his best foot forward and yes, he is mildly mentally retarded. But he was able to get by in school because he was well disciplined, well behaved, and these–kids sometimes fall through the cracks. He tried, he put his best foot forward, put the only proof before you that anybody has an opinion with certainty is Dr. McCoy's, is that he is mildly mentally retarded. Dr. Allen says–I can't tell you he is and I can't tell you that he is not, I don't know. That is what he said.

John is a young man of twenty-six years old, no doubt about that, and has a mental age of ten years and nine months, and I submit to you that our proof bears that out, and it is Dr. McCoy's computation of his mental age that you ought to consider. Dr. Allen's computation of mental age makes no sense, because someone who can barely function and someone with an IQ in the 30s cannot, they can't feed themselves, they can't wash themselves. But according to Dr. Allen's computation, if you live old enough you will be able to do that. Well, that is just not true. It doesn't make sense. It is not common sense. But Dr. McCoy's computation does make common sense and especially if you think about it. That mental age is about like a sixth grader. And remember, looking at John's records, that is about where he could function on the proficiency tests he couldn't go past that of the sixth to eighth grade level. He made his best grade in Agriculture classes where he could learn things by doing with his hands, by rote. But he never could do well in reading and spelling and so forth. And all of that is consistent with that mental age that Dr. McCoy found.

The capacity of John to appreciate the wrongfulness of his conduct or to conform his conduct within the requirements of law has been impaired by that mental retardation. And you ought to consider that. That is important when you are thinking about what an appropriate punishment is.

John assisted the authorities in locating the gun used in the crime. No question about that. He could have said-I am not telling you, I am not going to show you, you will have to get a search warrant, or he could have hidden it. None of that happened. He told them where it was, they went right to it and got it. And he ought to be given credit for that.

He is a Baptist, brought up in the Baptist church, his father is a Baptist preacher. No question about it. And he ought to be given credit for that.

He has been a hard worker and will continue to work in prison, and you don't have any reason to believe anything different but that he will continue to work hard. He always has, he always will. And you ought to consider that in the punishment, and you ought to give him credit for that.

He works well with his hands and is a good mechanic. No question about that. That has been proven, and that is something–another skill that can be used in the penitentiary, and he ought to be given credit for that.

And lastly, that he is a good neighbor. We all ought to give him credit for that life, and that's true.

Remember the test of what outweighs what. If you look at these and you say-well, it's a tie. Then your verdict would be life imprisonment. Because this one has to outweigh all of these. Remember that. That is what the law is. That is what the law is. This one circumstance has to outweigh all of the good things that he has done, and I submit to you that it doesn't, because this is not the appropriate kind of case for the death penalty.

You may also consider any lingering doubt you have about this case. You know, sometimes people get convicted wrong, when all of the evidence to a jury just like you seems conclusive, and you find beyond a reasonable doubt, and you have, and we accept that. We have. But then there is sometimes cases where there are five eyewitnesses that say a man did it, we had one in Tennessee, Doug Forbes, he was a postman. And that he spent five years in the penitentiary, and what happened? Later the real killer, the real rapist, I am sorry, confessed, and he was let out after five years. Any of us can make mistakes and you can only go by what evidence you see, I understand that. But if you have any lingering doubt at all, ladies and gentlemen, if we put him in prison for life, and later we find out that it was wrong, that somebody else confessed to doing it, we can get him out. If we strap him to the electric chair, and we electrocute him, there is nothing we can do about it. You can consider that, and I ask you, please to do so. Mercy.

One of the good things about our society as Americans is that we are merciful people, and you can consider mercy in this and I believe all of you are merciful. I wouldn't have picked you as jurors if I didn't believe it. And you can consider mercy for John Wallen in this case.

When you go back to the jury room, whatever you decide, each of you has to sign your name on it. Obviously because it is so important. I ask each of you, those that believe that life imprisonment is appropriate, if there is anybody that disagrees with you in the jury room, stick to your guns. Please, stick to your guns. Because the State cannot electrocute John Wallen unless it has all twelve names on that death verdict. Stick to your guns, please.

Ladies and gentlemen, his mother, his father, his girlfriend, his aunts, his sisters got up here and begged you to spare his life and now I am begging you, please, please make his punishment for the rest of his life in the State penitentiary.

Thank you, ladies and gentlemen.

END OF CLOSING ARGUMENT

In the penalty phase of a capital case, a lawyer may, as Darrow did, feel that it is appropriate to argue against the death penalty itself. His argument sets out the traditional arguments against capital punishment along with one that I feel is very compelling—that it is an attraction to deranged serial killers who are looking for notoriety and infamy.

One of the most commonly debated issues is whether capital punishment is a deterrent. Opponents of capital punishment argue that knowing the death penalty is a consequence for murder deters people from committing crime. Opponents of the death penalty argue that people who commit the kinds of heinous crimes who are today eligible for the death penalty do not think of the consequences before they commit their crimes. Murder rates studies in neighboring states such as Michigan and Ohio (Michigan does not have the death penalty and Ohio does) show murder rates to be very similar.

Opponents of the death penalty argue that restraint is absolute when one is executed. There is no argument against that proposition. Restraint, however, can be accomplished by imprisonment for life without parole.

Possibly the strongest argument for the death penalty is that of retribution, particularly for families of the victims. Where one stands on retribution and the kind of retribution that is appropriate for the state to administer is ultimately a moral decision the individual has to make. There are certainly those who believe in an eye for an eye and a tooth for a tooth and others who believe the state does not have the moral authority to kill someone for having been convicted of a crime.

There are also those who argue that the death penalty is necessary for economic reasons. They argue the state (and specifically the taxpayers) should not be responsible for keeping someone locked up for life. There are other studies, however, which show that it cost more to keep someone in the ultra maximum security facilities called death row and to pay for their appeals than it does to keep someone in the general population to serve a life sentence.

The economic issue can also be argued by those opposed to capital punishment because clearly poor people are much more likely to get the death penalty than those with the adequate resources to fund their defense.

Opponents of the death penalty also point out that the race of the defendant and the victim play a disproportionate role in deciding who will get the death penalty. Black defendants with white victims are much more likely than any other group to get the death penalty. Historically in the South, black defendants who raped white woman were by far the largest single category of those who were executed.

Geographics also figure into the death penalty. Proponents say that is appropriate because local communities should decide how to punish people who commit heinous crimes. Opponents of the death penalty say that geographics show that the death penalty is arbitrarily given. Within our state, it is no secret that some communities are much more likely to impose the death penalty than others.

It is also a fact that personalities play into whether or not the death penalty is imposed. The discretion of the prosecutor whether to seek the death penalty depends a lot on his own personal feelings. Who the defense lawyer is, who the judge is, and who the jury pool is also dictate the frequency with which the death penalty is imposed in a particular area.

One of the strongest arguments against capital punishment of late is that of actual innocence. It is no secret that our criminal justice system is fallible and does make mistakes. We certainly can never correct the mistake when we have executed a person. Advances in DNA have led to the release of many prisoners, including a number of those on death row, who are now known to be actually innocent of the crime.

The new argument that I advance for your consideration is whether the death penalty is an attractive nuisance. By using this tort term I apologize to my brothers and sisters in the civil bar and hope that I do not abuse it. There are, however, circumstances under which I submit the death penalty actually contributes to the heinous killing of innocent people.

Take the case of twisted, serial killers like Ted Bundy. Ted Bundy, as we know, went around the country strangling to death innocent co-eds at our colleges and universities. Ted Bundy attended college for a while and asked a lawyer friend of his in Colorado where he would go if he wanted to get the death penalty. For those who practice criminal law, it is no secret that the states which impose the death penalty with greatest frequency are Texas and Florida. We know that Ted Bundy went on to Florida where he finished his string of senseless and heinous murders of young college women. If Ted Bundy were not seeking the notoriety and infamy that the death penalty would bring him, would he have gone to Florida to continue his trail of horrible killings? For people like Ted Bundy, is the death penalty actually an attraction which gives them the kind of infamy and notoriety that they could never legitimately receive in any other way?

Another category of horrible killers for whom the death penalty may be an attraction is that of sick, fanatical madmen like Timothy McVeigh. People as twisted as he and as committed to fanatical violent causes often perceive themselves as martyrs. Witness the fact that McVeigh wants his execution to be televised nationwide. Remember that the Oklahoma City bombing was in revenge for the federal assault on the Branch Davidian compound in Waco, Texas. The bombing occurred on the anniversary of that assault. Do we want McVeigh's perceived martyrdom to encourage other sick fanatics to similarly avenge McVeigh's execution? Do we want to make martyrs out of foreign fanatics who hate the United

States and all it stands for? I submit that it may be better to imprison those people for life without parole. For some, that punishment is greater. There is a very real possibility that the denial of infamy is one of the reasons Tommy Burks' family asked the State of Tennessee not to seek the death penalty but to seek life without parole against Byron Looper. We know there are those who would rather die than continue to live in prison on death row. We read all the time about people wanting to give up their appeals, like Timothy McVeigh in order to be executed.

Would it not be better to keep these persons in prison for life without parole never to leave their cell with mandatory psychological, neurological and criminological studies being made on and about them? Such studies could help us understand what makes a person become a serial or fanatical killer of innocent people. Their twisted brains certainly are of little value after they are dead. While they are alive, however, we might learn much to help us and future generations spare the taking of innocent lives by studying the minds that we know have to be consumed with sick desires.

Darrow argues to the jury in Tennessee vs. John Thomas Scopes

CHAPTER 5

CLOSING ARGUMENT — ATTACKING THE STATE'S PSYCHIATRIST

When Clarence Darrow successfully argued for life for Nathan Leopold and Dickie Loeb, he was not hesitant to attack the state psychiatrist, Dr. Krohn. He was never hesitant, nor should we be, to go after an expert witness from the other side who has clearly shown bias and, as often is the case, the very profunctionary examination because he knows what result he is going to achieve before he starts.

Following the excerpt of Darrow's closing in Leopold and Loeb, is a closing argument I gave for a young man whose alias was John Smith. Joseph Daniel Carterman was clearly mentally ill. He had copied the Bible in long hand and left his mother's home for long periods of time without explanation. On the day in question, he rode his bicycle from Chattanooga, Tennessee to Knoxville, Tennessee, a distance of 110 miles. He went to a pizza parlor and asked where the restroom was when he went in. Though directed to the men's room, he went in to the women's room and stood in front of the mirror mumbling. He came out and went to the salad bar where one of the employees was cleaning. He dropped down on his knees and grabbed her crotch. He was somewhat smaller than her and ran. Fortunately the police found him before her boyfriend did. We offered only lay proof of his insanity. The State's psychologist did not do much of an examination, and his testimony showed it. In the closing argument we successfully convinced the jury that Daniel was insane at the time of the offense.

Excerpt of Darrow's closing argument in Leopold and Loeb

When [Dr. Krohn, prosecution psychiatrist] testified my mind carried me back to the time when I was a kid, which was some years ago, and we used to eat watermelons. I have seen little boys take a rind of watermelon and cover their whole faces with watermelon, eat it, devour it, and have the time of their lives, up to their ears in watermelon. And when I heard Dr. Krohn testify in this case, to take the blood of these two boys, I could see his mouth water with the joy it gave him, and he showed all the delight and pleasure of myself and my young companions when we ate watermelon. . . .

I can never imagine a real physician who cared for life or who thought of anything excepting cash, gloating over his testimony, as Dr. Krohn did in this case.

IN THE CRIMINAL COURT FOR KNOX COUNTY, DIVISION I

AT KNOXVILLE, TENNESSEE

STATE OF TENNESSEE	)	
	)	
VS.	)	CASE NO. *22374*
	)	
JOHN SMITH, ALIAS	)	
JOSEPH DANIEL CARTERMAN	)	

This case came on to be heard for trial and was heard on the 18th day of February, 1985, before the Honorable Richard R. Baumgartner, Judge, holding the Criminal Court Knox County, Division I, at Knoxville, Tennessee, when the following closing argument of defense counsel was had:

MR. TRANT: Ladies and gentlemen, I am not here today to ask you to excuse the conduct of this young man. He needs help, and the way that we make sure that he gets that help is to send him to a mental hospital, and the way that we do that is to reach the right verdict in this case that he is not guilty by reason of insanity.

Now, think about it. Mr. Jennings tries to say that, well, the issue of sanity has not been raised. Now, can you believe that? I mean, to hear his mom and his brother talk about the deterioration of his mental health over the past several years and to say that you should not even consider whether or not he was sane or insane at the time of this defense? Because he knows that, once you do that, then he has to prove to you beyond a reasonable doubt and to a moral certainty that he is sane, and he knows he can't do that. He knows he can't do that.

Now, let's look—I want to talk about Dr. Kronic first. We have a man who is an employee of the State of Tennessee who does an hour and a half examination of this young man, who gives him none of the recognized tests for determining sanity at the time of the offense, who I submit to you jumps to some conclusions; and then, when asked about things that he didn't know about, he said, "Yeah, those can be symptoms of mental illness. The laughing uncontrollably, that can be hallucination. The fascination with his body, yes, that is a symptom."

Think about that. Now, maybe in fairness to Dr. Kronic, maybe if he had known those things, he might have considered them, but he didn't. And he told you, well, it could be mental illness that could keep him from talking. But think about the important thing that he said, and that was, "I can't tell you within a reasonable degree of psychological certainty that he was sane at the time of the offense."

That is exactly what they have to prove and didn't. Their own witnesses, I can't tell you that. I can't tell you that." But that is what they have to prove. Now, let's look at the proof in this case, and let's look at this young man, whether he is well or whether he is sick.

Does a well young man go for walks—twenty-four-hour walks—time after time after time? Does a well young man pace around the house, say nothing, and then all of a sudden just start laughing at nothing time after time after time? Does a well young man sit down and copy things out of books, copy the Bible, copy the table of contents of scientific books for no apparent reason time after time after time?

Does a well young man become withdrawn, become afraid of his mother, blame his mother for what is going on? Does a well young man's grades drop in school time after time after time? Now, if he is so smart, so good at beating the system like Mr. Jennings says, why didn't he beat the system at school? Because he is sick. This young man is sick. He is mentally ill. There is no question about it.

Does a well young man on April 16, 1984, get on his bicycle and bike from Knoxville, Tennessee to Chattanooga, Tennessee?

MR. JENNINGS:	Your Honor, I object. There is no proof of that.
MR. TRANT:	Does a well young man—
	Your Honor, please, the last time—
THE COURT:	Well, all that—
MR. TRANT:	I am sorry.
THE COURT:	Well, all that they said was that he left his home on his bicycle. Of course, there wasn't any proof about how he definitely got there, but that is–go ahead—
MR. TRANT:	Thank you, Your Honor.
THE COURT:	—Mr. Trant.
MR. TRANT:	Does a well young man stop at a pizza place, go in, go up to the counter, start mumbling something about discounts, something about the bathroom, not looking the lady in the eye? And then does a well young man do exactly what he did at home, go into the bathroom, stare in the mirror for 10 to 15 minutes, went in the women's bathroom? And then does he go out for no reason—no reason—and briefly crouch down and touch the pants covering the genitals of this young lady here, saying nothing, not trying to take her clothes off, not pulling a weapon on her, not saying, "Come with me, not saying, "I am going to rape you," not saying anything?

And then she turns around to come after him. Now, I submit to you that he wasn't fleeing from the law. He was fleeing from Carla Finch. Carla Finch, who was about a head taller than him, was coming after him. I can't say that I blame her. He runs into the door. Then he gets out. He runs into a car, and he does what he has to do to get away from her, because she is after him. A mentally ill person can understand when somebody is after him.

So what does he do? Finally, she catches him. He hits her one time. He doesn't sit there and pound her. He gets away. But then, remember, it is four or five minutes before the policemen arrive on the scene, and then it is 20 or 30 minutes before he finds them. He has not gotten on his bike and driven away somewhere. He is still in the area, still in the area.

I submit to you what John Smith, Daniel Carterman, was doing in that restaurant was doing what he could do as a cry for help. That is what he was doing. He wasn't doing this for sexual gratification. I think part of Daniel Carterman knows he needs some help, and he did something to try to get some help.

Now, if John Smith, Daniel Carterman is as intelligent as Dr. Kronic says—and maybe he is—people can be mentally ill and be intelligent. I think history has shown that repeatedly. Then why would he give three different ages to the policeman? If he is so intelligent, why wouldn't he just clam up and not say anything to Dr. Kronic at all? Because he is not being evasive. It is because he is mentally ill.

Now, you have two choices in this case. You can believe what David Jennings says, believe that he has carried his proof beyond a reasonable doubt to a moral certainty in proving this young man to be sane, and you can find him guilty, and he can be sent to the penitentiary. I ask you what kind of help he is going to get there.

Or—or you can hold the State of Tennessee to its burden, its burden that it has to prove to you beyond a reasonable doubt and to a moral certainty that at the time of this offense that he was sane, something they have not done. They have not introduced a witness who has been able to do that.

All the evidence has been to the contrary, that his sanity had been deteriorated for years from people that didn't meet with him an hour and a half, people that lived with him—his mom, his brother—who saw him day after day after day, who saw his condition deteriorate. You can listen to them. They know better than anybody what his behavior was like.

And then ask yourself: Can my mind rest easy that the State has proven him sane beyond a reasonable doubt? And, if it cannot, then your verdict shall be not guilty by reason of insanity, and he will be automatically detained under the law and will be sent to a mental hospital where I submit to you he will spend longer than if you send him to the penitentiary. He will be evaluated there, and he will be treated.

That is the way to protect society; it is the way to protect Daniel Carterman is to see that he gets some help. It is the right thing to do, the just thing to do in this case, and I ask you to do that. Thank you very much.

(END OF REQUESTED TRANSCRIPT OF EVIDENCE)

The all-white Detroit jury that acquitted Henry Sweet

CHAPTER 6

CLOSING ARGUMENT/BEATING THE MURDER RAP

"I never killed a man, but I have read many obituaries with a lot of pleasure"
Clarence Darrow

Convincing a jury that your client is not guilty of murder when the police, prosecutor and probably the judge believe to the contrary, is never easy. This is particularly true when your client actually did the killing.

The closing argument of Darrow in State of Michigan v. Henry Sweet presents a compelling example of how to convince a jury that your client is not guilty when, he in fact, committed the killing.

What follows is a transcript of my closing argument in the State of Tennessee vs. Johnny Joe Crass, Jr. Johnny had previously been convicted of the murder but had the conviction set aside when the court found that his trial counsel was ineffective. I was asked to represent him in the retrial. Our theory was self defense, and the jury accepted that theory by finding Johnny not guilty.

This case also illustrates how the use of a prop can be very effective. I obtained from a client's brother, who is a wholesale knife distributor, a replica of the knife which OJ Simpson bought in Los Angeles and probably used to kill Nicole Simpson and Ronald Goldman. The Stiletto knife with a blade of over six inches drew a marked contrast between the small pocket knife which Johnny Joe Crass used in our case.

Like in Sweet, the jury found Johnny Joe Crass not guilty of murder.

Closing Argument of Clarence Darrow in the case of State of Michigan v. Henry Sweet

If the Court please, Gentlemen of the Jury: You have listened so long and patiently that I do not know whether you are able to stand much more. I want to say, however, that while I have tried a good many cases in the forty-seven or forty-eight years that I have lived in court houses, that in one way this has been one of the pleasantest trials I have ever been in. The kindness and the consideration of the Court is such as to make it easy for everybody, and I have seldom found as courteous, gentlemanly and kindly opponents as I have had in this case. I appreciate their friendship. Lawyers are apt to look at cases from different standpoints, and I sometimes find it difficult to understand how a lawyer on the other side can think as he thinks and say what he says. I, being an extremely reasonable man and entirely free from all kinds of prejudices myself, find this hard to comprehend.

I shall begin about where my friend Mr. Moll [*Assistant Wayne County Prosecutor Lester Moll: ed.*] began yesterday. He says lightly, gentlemen, that this isn't a race question. This is a murder case. We don't want any prejudice; we don't want the other side to have any. Race and color have nothing to do with this case. This is a case of murder.

Now, let's see; I am going to try to be as fair as I can with you gentlemen; still I don't mind being watched at that. I just want you to give such consideration to what I say as you think it is worth. I insist that there is nothing but prejudice in this case; that if it was reversed and eleven white men had shot and killed a black while protecting their home and their lives against a mob of blacks, nobody would have dreamed of having them indicted. I know what I am talking about, and so do you. They would have been given medals instead.

Eleven colored men and one woman are in this indictment, tried by twelve jurors, gentlemen. Every one of you are white, aren't you? At least you all think so. We haven't one colored man on this jury. We couldn't get one. One was called and he was disqualified. You twelve white men are trying a colored man on race prejudice. Now, let me ask you whether you are not prejudiced. I want to put this square to you, gentlemen. I haven't any doubt but that everyone of you are prejudiced against colored people. I want you to guard against it. I want you to do all you can to be fair in this case, and I believe you will. A number of you people have answered the question that you are acquainted with colored people. One juror I have in mind, who is sitting here, said there were two or three families living on the street in the block where he lives, and he had lived there for a year or more, but he didn't know their names and had never met them. Some of the rest of you said that you had employed colored people to work for you, are even employing them now. All right.

You have seen some of the colored people in this case. They have been so far above the white people that live at the corner of Garland and Charlevoix [*in eastern Detroit, where the shooting occurred: ed.*] that they can't be compared, intellectually, morally and physically, and you know it. How many of you jurors, gentlemen, have ever had a colored person visit you in your home? How many of you have ever visited in their homes? How many of you have invited them to dinner at your house? Probably not one of you. Now, why, gentlemen?

There isn't one of you men but what you know just from the witnesses you have seen in this case that there are colored people who are intellectually the equal of all of you. Am I right? Colored people living right here in the City of Detroit are intellectually the equals and some of them superior to most of us. Is that true? Some of them are people of more character and learning than most of us. I have a picture in my mind of the first witness we put on the stand—Mrs. Spalding. Modest, intelligent, beautiful; the beauty in her face doesn't come from powder or paint, or any artificial means, but has to come from within; kindly, human feeling. You couldn't forget her. I couldn't forget her. You seldom have seen anybody of her beauty and her appearance. She has some colored blood in her veins. Compare her with the teacher who for ten years has taught high school on what she called the corner of Garland and "Gote" Street. Compare the two.

Now, why don't you individually, and why don't I, and why doesn't every white person whose chances have been greater and whose wealth is larger, associate with them? There is only one reason, and that is prejudice. Can you give any other reason for it? They would be intellectual companions. They have good manners. They are clean. They are all of them clean enough to wait on us, but not clean enough to associate with. Is there any reason in the world why we don't associate with them excepting prejudice? Still none of us want to be prejudiced. I think not one man of this jury wants to be prejudiced. It is forced into us almost from our youth until somehow or other we feel we are superior to these people who have black faces.

Now, gentlemen, I say you are prejudiced. I fancy everyone of you are, otherwise you would have some companions amongst these colored people. You will overcome it, I believe, in the trial of this case. But they tell me there is no race prejudice, and it is plain nonsense, and nothing else. Who are we, anyway? A child is born into this world without any knowledge of any sort. He has a brain which is a piece of putty; he inherits nothing in the way of knowledge or of ideas. If he is white, he knows nothing about color. He has no antipathy to the black.

The black and the white both will live together and play together, but as soon as the baby is born we begin giving him ideas. We begin planting seeds in his mind. We begin telling him he must do this and he must not do that. We tell him about race and social equality and the thousands of things that men talk about until he grows up. It has been trained into us, and you, gentlemen, bring that feeling into this jury box, and that feeling which is a part of your life long training.

You need not tell me you are not prejudiced. I know better. We are not very much but a bundle of prejudices anyhow. We are prejudiced against other peoples' color. Prejudiced against other men's religion; prejudiced against other peoples' politics. Prejudiced against peoples' looks. Prejudiced about the way they dress. We are full of prejudices. You can teach a man anything beginning with the child; you can make anything out of him, and we are not responsible for it. Here and there some of us haven't any prejudices on some questions, but if you look deep enough you will find them; and we all know it.

All I hope for, gentlemen of the jury, is this: That you are strong enough, and honest enough, and decent enough to lay it aside in this case and decide it as you ought to. And I say, there is no man in Detroit that doesn't know that these defendants, everyone of them, did right. There isn't a man in Detroit who doesn't know that the defendant did his duty, and that this case is an attempt to send him and his companions to prison because they defended their constitutional rights. It is a wicked attempt, and you are asked to be a party to it. You know it. I don't need to talk to this jury about the facts in this case. There is no man who can read or can understand that does not know the facts. Is there prejudice in it?

Now, let's see. I don't want to lean very much on your intelligence. I don't need much. I just need a little. Would this case be in this court if these defendants were not black? Would we be standing in front of you if these defendants were not black? Would anybody be asking you to send a boy to prison for life for defending his brother's home and protecting his own life, if his face wasn't black? What were the people in the neighborhood of Charlevoix and Garland Streets doing on that fatal night? There isn't a child that doesn't know. Have you any doubt as to why they were there?

Was Mr. Moll right when he said that color has nothing to do with the case? There is nothing else in this case but the feeling of prejudice which has been carefully nourished by the white man until he doesn't know that he has it himself. While I admire and like my friend Moll very much, I can't help criticizing his argument. I suppose I may say what old men are apt to say, in a sort of patronizing way, that his zeal is due to youth and inexperience. That is about all we have to brag about as we get older, so we ought to be permitted to do that. Let us look at this case.

Mr. Moll took particular pains to say to you, gentlemen, that these eleven people here are guilty of murder; he calls this a cold-blooded, deliberate and premeditated murder; that is, they were there to kill. That was their purpose. Eleven, he said. I am not going to discuss the case of all of them just now, but I am starting where he started. He doesn't want any misunderstanding.

Amongst that eleven is Mrs. Sweet. The wife of Dr. Sweet, she is a murderer, gentlemen? The State's Attorney said so, and the Assistant State's Attorney said so. The State's Attorney would have to endorse it because he, himself, stands by what his assistant says. Pray, tell me what has Mrs. Sweet done to make her a murderer? She is the wife of Dr. Sweet. She is the mother of his little baby. She left the child at her mother's home while she moved into this highly cultured community near Goethe Street. Anyhow, the baby was to be safe; but she took her own chance, and she didn't have a gun; none was provided for her. Brother Toms drew from the witnesses that there were ten guns, and ten men. He didn't leave any for her. Maybe she had a pen knife, but there is no evidence on that question. What did she do, gentlemen? She is put down here as a murderer. She wasn't even upstairs. She didn't even look out of a window. She was down in the back kitchen cooking a ham to feed her family and friends, and a white mob came to drive them out of their home before the ham was served for dinner. She is a murderer, and all of these defendants who were driven out of their home must go to the penitentiary for life if you can find twelve jurors somewhere who have enough prejudice in their hearts, and hatred in their minds.

Now, that is this case, gentlemen, and that is all there is to this case. Take the hatred away, and you have nothing left. Mr. Moll says that this is a case between Breiner [Leon Breiner, the victim: ed.] and Henry Sweet.

Mr. Moll: No, I did not say any such thing.

Mr. Darrow: Well, let me correct it. He says that he holds a brief for Breiner. That is right; isn't it.

Mr. Moll: That is right.

Mr. Darrow: Well, I will put it just as it is, he holds a brief for Breiner, this Prosecuting Attorney. He is wrong. If he holds a brief for Breiner, he should throw it in the stove. It has no place in a court of justice. The question here is whether these defendants or this defendant is guilty of murder. It has nothing to do with Breiner.

He says that I wiggled and squirmed every time they mentioned Breiner. Well, now, I don't know. Did I? Maybe I did. I didn't know it. I have been around court rooms so long that I fancy I could listen to anything without moving a hair. Maybe I couldn't. And, I rather think my friend is pretty wise. He said that I don't like to hear them talk about Breiner. I don't, gentlemen, and I might have shown it. This isn't the first case I was ever in. I don't like to hear the State's Attorney talk about the blood of a victim. It has such a mussy sound. I wish they would leave it out. I will be frank with you about it. I don't think it has any place in a case. I think it tends to create prejudice and feeling and it has no place, and it is always dangerous. And perhaps—whether I showed it or not, my friend read my mind. I don't like it.

Now, gentlemen, as he talked about Breiner, I am going to talk about him, and it isn't easy, either. It isn't easy to talk about the dead, unless you "slobber" over them and I am not going to "slobber" over Breiner. I am going to tell you the truth about it. Why did he say that he held a brief for Breiner, and ask you to judge between Breiner and Henry Sweet? You know why he said it. To get a verdict, gentlemen. That is why he said it. Had it any place in this case? Henry Sweet never knew that such a man lived as Breiner. Did he? He didn't shoot at him. Somebody shot out into that crowd and Breiner got it. Nobody had any feeling against him.

But who was Breiner, anyway? I will tell you who he was. I am going to measure my words when I state it, and I am going to make good before I am through in what I say. Who was he? He was a conspirator in as foul a conspiracy as was ever hatched in a community; in a conspiracy to drive from their homes a little family of black people and not only that, but to destroy these blacks and their home. Now, let me see whether I am right. What do we know of Breiner? He lived two blocks from the Sweet home. On the 14th day of July, seven hundred people met at the schoolhouse and the schoolhouse was too small, and they went out into the yard. This schoolhouse was across the street from the Sweet house.

Every man, in that community knew all about it. Every man in that community understood it. And in that schoolhouse a man rose and told what they had done in his community; that by main force they had driven Negro families from their homes, and that when a Negro moved to Garland Street, their people would be present to help. That is why Mr. Breiner came early to the circus on the 9th. He went past that house, back and forth, two or three times that night. Any question about that? Two or, three times that night he wandered past that house. What was he doing? "Smoking his pipe." What were the rest of them doing? They were a part of a mob and they had no rights, and the Court will tell you so, I think. And, if he does, gentlemen, it is your duty to accept it.

Was Breiner innocent? If he was every other man there was innocent. He left his home. He had gone two or three times down to the corner and back. He had come to Dove's steps where a crowd had collected and peacefully pulled out his pipe and begun to smoke until the curtain should be raised. You know it. Why was he there? He was there just the same as the Roman populace were wont to gather at the Colosseum where they brought out the slaves and the gladiators and waited for the lions to be unloosed. That is why he was there. He was there waiting to see these black men driven from their homes, and you know it; peacefully smoking his pipe, and as innocent a man as ever scuttled a ship. No innocent people were there. What else did Breiner do? He sat there while boys came and stood in front of him not five feet away, and stoned these black people's homes, didn't he? Did he raise his hand? Did he try to protect any of them? No, no. He was not there for that. He was there waiting for the circus to begin.

Gentlemen, it is a reflection upon anybody's intelligence to say that everyone did not know why this mob was there. You know! Everyone of you know why. They came early to take their seats at the ringside. Didn't they? And Breiner sat at one point where the stones were thrown, didn't he? Was he a member of that mob? Gentlemen, that mob was bent not only on making an assault upon the rights of the owners of that house, not only making an assault upon their persons and their property, but they were making an assault on the constitution and the laws of the nation, and the state under which they live. They were like Samson in the temple, seeking to tear down the pillars of the structure. So that blind prejudices and their bitter hate would rule supreme in the City of Detroit. Now, that was the case.

Gentlemen, does anybody need to argue to you as to why those people were there? Was my friend Moll even intelligent when he told you that this was a neighborly crowd? I wonder if he knows you better than I do. I hope not. A neighborly crowd? A man who comes to your home and puts a razor across your windpipe, or who meets you on the street and puts a dagger through your heart is as much a neighbor as these conspirators and rioters were who drove these black people from their home. Neighbors, eh? Visiting? Bringing them greetings and good cheer! Our people were newcomers. They might have needed their larder stocked. It was a hot night. The crowd probably brought them ice cream and soda, and possibly other cold drinks. Neighbors? Gentlemen,—neighbors? They were neighbors in the same sense that a nest of rattlesnakes are neighbors when you accidentally put your foot upon them. They are neighbors in the sense that a viper is a neighbor when you warm it in your bosom and it bites you. And every man who knows anything, about this case knows it. You know what the purpose was.

Where did you get that fool word "neighborly?" I will tell you where he got it. A witness on our side, a reporter on the News, said that he parked his automobile upon the street. People around there call it "Gothy" Street but intelligent people call it "Goethe" Street; and then he walked down Garland. And, as he started down the street, he observed that the crowd was plainly made up largely of neighbors and the people who lived there, a neighborly, visiting crowd. As he got down toward Charlevoix he found the crowd changing—the whole aspect has changed. They were noisy and riotous and turbulent. Now, gentlemen, am I stating it right? Or am I stating it wrong? Is it an insult to one's intelligence to say those were neighbors? They knew why they were there. They had been getting ready a long time for this welcome. They were neighbors in the sense that an undertaker is a neighbor when he comes to carry out a corpse, and that is what they came for, but it was the wrong corpse. That is all.

Now, let us see who were there and how many were there. Gentlemen, my friend said that he wasn't going to mince matters. I think I will, because I know the prejudice is the other way. You can pick twelve men in these black faces that are watching your deliberations and have throughout all these weary days, and with them I would not need to mince matters; but I must be very careful not to shock your sensibilities. I must state just as much or as near the facts as I dare to state without shocking you and be fair to my client.

It was bad enough for a mob, by force and violation of law, to attempt to drive these people from their house, but gentlemen, it is worse to send them to prison for life for defending their home. Think of it. That is this case. Are we human? Hardly. Did the witnesses for the State appearing here tell the truth? You know they did not. I am not going to analyze the testimony of every one of them. But they did not tell the truth and they did not mean to tell the truth.

Let me ask you this question, gentlemen: Mr. Moll says that these colored people had a perfect right to live in that house. Still he did not waste any sympathy on the attempt to drive them out. He did not say it was an outrage to molest them. Oh, no, he said they had a perfect right to live in that house. But the mob met there to drive them out. That is exactly what they did, and they have lied, and lied, and lied to send these defendants to the penitentiary for life, so that they will not go back to their home.

Now, you know that the mob met there for that purpose. They violated the constitution and the law, they violated every human feeling, and threw justice and mercy and humanity to the winds, and they made a murderous attack upon their neighbor because his face was black. Which is the worse, to do that or lie about it? In describing this mob, I heard the word "few" from the State's witnesses so many times that I could hear it in my sleep, and I presume that when I am dying I will hear that "few", "few", "few" stuff that I heard in Detroit from people who lied and lied and lied. What was this "few?" And who were they, or how did they come there? I can't tell you about everyone of these witnesses, but I can tell you about some of them. Too many. I can't even carry all of their names in my mind and I don't want to. There are other things more interesting; bugs, for instance. Anything is more interesting to carry in your mind, than the names of that bunch, and yet I am going to say something for them, too, because I know something about human nature and life; and I want to be fair, and if I did not want to, I think perhaps it would pay me to be.

Are the people who live around the corner of Charlevoix and Garland worse than other people? There isn't one of you who doesn't know that they lied. There isn't one of you who does not know that they tried to drive those people out and now are trying to send them to the penitentiary so that they can't move back; all in violation of the law, and are trying to get you to do the job. Are they worse than other people? I don't know as they are. How much do you know about prejudice? Race prejudice. Religious prejudice. These feelings that have divided men and caused them to do the most terrible things. Prejudices have burned men at the stake, broken them on the rack, torn every joint apart, destroyed people by the million. Men have done this on account of some terrible prejudice which even now is reaching out to undermine this republic of ours and to destroy the freedom that has been the most cherished part of our institutions.

These witnesses honestly believe that they are better than blacks. I do not. They honestly believe that it is their duty to keep colored people out. They honestly believe that the blacks are an inferior race and yet they look at themselves, I don't know how they can. If they had one colored family up there, some of the neighbors might learn how to pronounce "Goethe." It would be too bad to spread a little culture in that vicinity. They might die. They are possessed with that idea and that fanaticism, and when people are possessed with that they are terribly cruel. They don't stand alone. Others have done the same thing. Others will do the same thing so long as this weary old world shall last. They may do it again, but, gentlemen, they ought not to ask you to do it for them. That is a pretty dirty job to turn over to a jury, and they ought not to expect you to do it.

Now, what did this "neighborly" crowd do, anyway? How many people were up there around Sweet's home? It was up to the State to bring all the people who knew about it. They had the first call and brought in some of the witnesses that knew about the case. They didn't find this honest, old German woman. They didn't find the reporter or newspaper man who worked for the *Detroit Daily News*. They didn't find the man who kept the tire store. Well, now, why didn't they?

I will say in my dealings with these prosecuting attorneys, that they have been perfectly fair about most matters during this trial. But, still, why did they leave out these witnesses? They were on the spot when it all happened. There are three righteous white people. I am a little rusty on the Bible, but perhaps you can correct me. Sodom and Gomorrah would have been saved if ten righteous men could have been found. If Sodom and Gomorrah could have been saved by ten, the corner of Charlevoix and Garland should have been saved by three.

Was there a crowd at that corner on that fatal night? Let me see what their witnesses say, if we can find out. Not one of them has told the truth, excepting as we dragged it from them. Mr. Dove lives right across the street from the Sweet house. He said he got home from his work and went out on his porch, and his wife and baby went with him. And there were two other people upstairs, and they were all there present at roll call, not only on the 9th but on the 8th. It was a warm evening and they got there in time for the shooting.

How hard it was to pry out of them that they went there on account of the colored people who had moved in across the way! You people are not lawyers. You do not know how hard it was to make them admit the truth. It is harder to pull the truth out of a reluctant witness than to listen to them lie. They were there on the porch for everything on earth except to see the slaughter. Still, they finally admitted that curiosity took them there, just curiosity. Curiosity over what? A black man had driven up to the house two small trucks containing a bed and a stove and a few chairs and a few clothes, and he was going to live in that community. That is why their witnesses went to that corner that night and reluctantly they admitted it.

Dove said that there were about ten or fifteen people in front of his house, and that Leon Breiner was sitting there on the lawn; and a number of other people standing there, too. Mrs. Dove said there were two over there and that she did not see Breiner, or anybody else, and the people upstairs weren't there, and the two roomers weren't there, although all of them have testified that they were present.

Here is another witness, Abbie Davis. She testified that she went down around the corner where everybody else went; we have had about ten or fifteen who went around that corner and each one said that no one else was there. She said, as I remember it, there were probably about twenty people on the street. And I asked: How, many in front of the Dove house? She didn't see any, though she was right across the street.

Let us take the corner of Charlevoix, where the school house stands, with the Sweet house on the other side. How many were there? Schuknecht, the officer [*Norton Schuknecht, a witness for the prosecution: ed.*], said that he stood on that corner all the evening. Schuknecht said that fifteen or twenty were standing there, and some other witnesses put it higher.

Miss Stowell,—Miss Stowell—do you see her? I do. S-t-o-w-e-1-1. You remember, gentlemen, that she spelled it for us. I can spell that in my sleep, too. I can spell it backwards. Well, let me recall her to you. She teaches school at the corner of Garland and "Gother" Street; fifteen years a high school teacher, and, in common with all the other people in the community, she called it "Gother" Street.

She came down to the apartment building, opposite the Sweet house that night to see about a picnic. She left just before the picnic began. She said she sat on the porch with Draper and his wife and made arrangements for the children to go to the picnic and she thought their boy was there, too.

Now, you remember Draper. Draper was a long, lean, hungry-looking duck. . . . He said he paced up and down in front of his house. He didn't see much of anything. I asked him where his boy was. Well, he thought his boy was part of the time out on that porch. Were you there? "No." Was your wife there? "No." Now, part of the time the boy was there. Well, now, Miss S-t-o-w-e-1–1 said that they were all there. She was there all right. Nobody was on the street in front of them. She sat right there.

And they called this fellow Belcher, the man who is so good to his wife. His wife had gone away—not for good—either for her good or his—to visit a sick friend that belonged to her lodge. And, as soon as she got out of the house Belcher started down to the corner across from the Sweet house and got restless and uneasy. Maybe he is telling the truth. I have a theory that might account for his telling the truth, but it is not the theory of the State. He paced up and down the block for half an hour looking over the street cars to see if, perchance, his wandering wife might return. She was accustomed to going out of nights, and the cars stopped at their door. It wasn't dark. The corner of Garland and Charlevoix is inhabited by very fine people who have an "improvement club" so as to keep it in proper condition for their children. I don't see why he was so restless about his wife; whatever it was, for more than half an hour, he was pacing back and forth; probably nearer an hour. He didn't see anybody else. He didn't see Draper.

He did see a policemen, but that is all; but, Miss S-t-o-w-e-1–1 didn't see him. Didn't see anything, but looked over at the other side to the schoolhouse yard, and what did she see? "Well, there were fifty or one hundred people around there." So, I don't know as I should complain so much about her. She came nearer to telling the truth about that than any other witness called by the State; a good deal nearer. She looked across the street and saw fifty or one hundred people, but she saw nobody on the sidewalk and it was seething with people who weren't even there, and when she went away she didn't look around the corners, and didn't know who were there. Wonderful witness, that woman.

Are there any two of their witnesses that have agreed on any fact? She says fifty or one hundred. What did the policeman say? There were about eight policemen standing around there to protect a colored family. Two of them were from Tennessee. That ought to have helped some. I don't know where the rest came from. Some of them seemed to come from some institution, judging by the way they talked. Do you remember the fellow that said he was parading all the evening along the one sidewalk next to his house? Right along here. Didn't see anybody. Didn't know whether anybody was over there in the schoolhouse-yard, and he said "there might have been four." Now, he is one, isn't he?

Here is another policeman, parading all the evening on this short beat. He came pretty nearly down to the corner. Nobody was on this corner. Was there anybody on the schoolhouse-yard? "There might have been four." Four, gentlemen. I wouldn't say this man lied. It takes some mentality to lie. An idiot can't lie. It takes mentality because it implies a design, and those two people had no design or anything else. Now, I won't say the same about Schuknecht. He has some mentality; some; just some. He said "there were probably one hundred and fifty around there." The next man—what is the name of the next policeman?

Mr. Toms [*Wayne County Prosecutor Robert M. Toms: ed.*]: Schellenberger [*Paul Schellenberger, also a witness for the prosecution: ed.*].

Mr. Darrow: Schellenberger. He said "there were forty or fifty," but he finally admitted that he said "one hundred and fifty" on the former trial. You can fix it the way you want it. Let me tell you this: Every witness the State put on told how the policemen were always keeping the crowd moving, didn't they? They were always driving people along and not permitting them to congregate, didn't they? Who were these people and where did they come from? No two witnesses on the part of the State have agreed about anything.

Let me give you another illustration of the wonderful mathematical geniuses who testified in this case. Let me refer to my friend, Abbie. I asked her this, did you belong to the improvement club? Yes. After a long time I brought out of her why she joined it. I asked: Did you go to that meeting at the corner of Charlevoix and Garland in the Howe School? "Yes." What was it about? "Don't know." Why did you go? "To find out." Did you find out? "No." Did you ask anybody? "No." How many were there? "About forty. I passed through the hall and then went outside. "Why? "Don't know." Did the crowd go out because there wasn't room for you. "Don't think so."

And then comes another busy lady, from just south of the schoolhouse. A typical club lady. A lady with a club—for Negroes. Now, what did she say? She is a wonder. I can see her now. That is the second time I have seen her, too. It would be terrible if I didn't have a chance to see her again. She went up there. Why? "Looking for my girl." Yes? I will mention about that girl. How many people did you see? "Oh, not many, a few around the corner." You belong to the Improvement Club? "Yes." Were you there to that meeting at the schoolhouse? "Yes." What was it about? "I don't know." Who spoke? "I don't know." What did they say? "I don't know." Nobody knows anything except one man and we pried that out of him. How many were there? "About forty." Did they adjourn later on? "Yes." Did you go out? "Yes." Didn't stay long.

Now they put another witness on the stand. Everybody in that vicinity belonged to the improvement club. I am going to mention this again, but I just want to speak about one thing in connection with that club. Mr. Andrews came here, and you remember my prying-out and surprising myself with my good luck, because when a lawyer gets something he wants, he doesn't at all feel that he was clever. He just worms around until he gets it, that's all. I asked:—Did you belong? He said he did. How many were at the meeting of the Improvement Club at the schoolhouse? "Oh, seven or eight hundred." That is their witness. They began in the schoolhouse and there wasn't room enough to hold them, and they went out in the yard. Now, these two noble ladies, mothers, looking for their daughters, they said "forty."

What did the speaker at the meeting say? "Well, one of them was very radical." He was? "Yes." What did he say? "He said he advocated violence. They told what they had done up there on Tireman Street, where they had driven Dr. Carter [*scil.; actually Dr. Alexander Turner: ed.*] out, and they wouldn't have him, and he said, whenever you undertake to do something with this Negro-question down here, we will support you." Gentlemen, are you deaf or dumb or blind, or just prejudiced, which means all three of them? No person with an ounce of intelligence could have any doubt about the facts in this case. This man says "seven or eight hundred" when these women say "forty." Another witness called by them said "five hundred." Andrews was the only man who testified as to who spoke at the meeting, or what he said; not another one. Did they lie? Yes, they lied, and you know they lied.

On the eve of the Sweet family moving into their home, and on the corner of the street where their home was located and in a public schoolhouse, not in the South but in Detroit. Six or seven hundred neighbors in this community listened to a speaker advocating the violation of the constitution and the laws, and calling upon the people to assemble with violence and force and drive these colored people from their homes. Seven hundred people there, and only one man told it.

Let me say something else about it, gentlemen. There were present at that meeting two detectives, sent by the Police Department to make a report. Officer Schuknecht said that he had heard about the formation of that "Improvement Club" and the calling of that meeting, and the purchase of that house by colored people, and he wanted to watch it. So he sent two detectives there. They heard this man make a speech that would send any black man to jail, that would have sent any political crusader to jail. They heard the speaker urge people to make an assault upon life and property; to violate the constitution and the law; to take things in their own hands and promise that an organization would stand back of them.

Why was he not arrested? Gentlemen, in a schoolyard paid for by your taxes; paid for by the common people, of every color, and every nationality, and every religion, that man stood there and harangued a mob and urged them to violence and crime in the presence of the officers of this city, and nothing was done about it. Didn't everybody in the community know it? Everybody! Didn't Schuknecht know it? He sent the detective there for that purpose. And what else did Andrews say? He said the audience applauded this mad and criminal speech, and he applauded, too.

And yet, you say that eleven poor blacks penned in a house for two days, with a surging mob around them, and knowing the temper of that community; and knowing all about what had happened in the past; reading the Mayor's proclamation, and seeing who was there, and knowing what occurred in the schoolhouse, waiting through the long night of the 8th and through the day of the 9th, walled in with the mob into the night of the 9th, until the stones fell on the roof, and windows were knocked out; and yet, gentlemen, you are told that they should have waited until their blood should be shed, even until they were dead, and liberty should be slain with them. How long, pray, must an intelligent American citizen wait in the City of Detroit, with all this history before them? And, then, gentlemen, after all that, these poor blacks are brought back into a court of justice and twelve jurors are asked to send them to prison for life.

I want to talk to you a little more about who was around that house, and why, and what they were doing, and how many there were. You may remember a man named Miller. This man Miller expressed it pretty well. I suppose I prodded him quite a bit. I asked—what was the organization for? "Oh, we want to protect the place." Against what? "Oh, well, generally." You can't make it more definite? "Yes, against undesirables." Who do you mean by "undesirables?" "Oh, people we don't want," and so on and so forth. Finally, he said, "against Negroes." I said: Anybody else? He thought awhile, and he said: "Well, against Eyetalians." He didn't say 'Italians.' He hadn't got that far along yet, but he said 'Eye-talians.' Of course, there was a Syrian merchant running the store on the corner, so Syrians evidently didn't count. By the way, we haven't seen that Syrian or heard from him. He must have done a fine business that night. He should have seen something. They were not prejudiced much about Syrians. They want to keep it American, Miller says. I asked him who the undesirables were, and the first are Negroes, and the second, Eye-talians.

Well, now, gentlemen, just by the way of passing, words are great things, you know. You hear some fellow who wants more money than you want, and he calls himself a one-hundred percent American. Probably he doesn't know what the word American means. But he knows what he wants. You hear some fellow who wants something else talking about Americanism. I don't know where Miller came from; about how early or how late an arrival he is in America. The only real Americans that I know about are the Indians, and we killed most of them and pensioned the rest.

I guess that the ancestors of my clients got here long before Miller's did. They have been here for more than three hundred years; before the Pilgrims landed, the slave ships landed, gentlemen. They are Americans and have given life and blood on a thousand different kinds of fields for America and have given their labor for nothing, for America. They are Americans. Mr. Miller doesn't know it. He thinks he is the only kind of American. The Negroes and Eye-talians don't count. Of course, he doesn't like them. Mr. Miller doesn't know that it was an Eye-talian that discovered this land of ours. Christopher Columbus was an 'Eye-talian,' but he isn't good enough to associate with Miller. None of the people of brains and courage and intelligence, unless they happen to live around those four corners, are good enough, and there are no brains and intelligence, and so forth, to spare around those corners. If there ever was they have been spared. These are the kind of prejudices that make up the warp and woof of this case.

Gentlemen, lawyers are very intemperate in their statements. My friend, Moll, said that my client here was a coward. A coward, gentlemen. Here, he says, were a gang of gun men, and cowards—shot Breiner through the back. Nobody saw Breiner, of course. If he had his face turned toward the house, while he was smoking there, waiting for the shooting to begin, it wasn't our fault. It wouldn't make any difference which way he turned. I suppose the bullet would have killed him just the same, if he had been in the way of it. If he had been at home, it would not have happened.

Who are the cowards in this case? Cowards, gentlemen! Eleven people with black skins, eleven people, gentlemen, whose ancestors did not come to America because they wanted to, but were brought here in slave ships, to toil for nothing, for the whites—whose lives have been taken in nearly every state in the Union,—they have been victims of riots all over this land of the free. They have had to take what is left after everybody else has grabbed what he wanted. The only place where he has been put in front is on the battle field. When we are fighting we give him a chance to die, and the best chance. But, everywhere else, he has been food for the flames, and the ropes, and the knives, and the guns and hate of the white, regardless of law and liberty, and the common sentiments of justice that should move men. Were they cowards? No, gentlemen, they may have been gun men. They may have tried to murder, but they were not cowards.

Eleven people, knowing what it meant, with the history of the race behind them, with the picture of Detroit in front of them; with the memory of Turner and Bristol [*Alexander Turner and Vollington Bristol, two Blacks driven out of their homes earlier in the summer of 1925: ed.*]; with the Mayor's proclamation still fresh on paper [*see below in Darrow's conclusion: ed.*], with the knowledge of shootings and killings and insult and injury without end, eleven of them go into a house, gentlemen, with no police protection, in the face of a mob, and the hatred of a community, and take guns and ammunition and fight for their rights, and for your rights and for mine, and for the rights of every being that lives. They went in and faced a mob seeking to tear them to bits. Call them something besides cowards.

The cowardly curs were in the mob gathered there with the backing of the law. A lot of children went in front and threw the stones. They stayed for two days and two nights in front of this home and by their threats and assault were trying to drive the Negroes out. Those were the cowardly curs, and you know it. I suppose there isn't any ten of them that would come out in the open daylight against those ten. Oh, no, gentlemen, their blood is too pure for that. They can only act like a band of coyotes baying some victim who has no chance.

And then my clients are called cowards. All right, gentlemen, call them something else. These blacks have been called many names along down through the ages, but there have been those through the sad years who believed in justice and mercy and charity and love and kindliness, and there have been those who believed that a black man should have some rights, even in a country where he was brought in chains. There are those even crazy enough to hope and to dream that sometime he will come from under this cloud and take his place amongst the people of the world. If he does, it will be through his courage and his culture. It will be by his intelligence and his scholarship and his effort, and I say, gentlemen of the jury, no honest, right feeling man, whether on a jury, or anywhere else, would place anything in his way in this great struggle behind him and before him.

Now, let us return to the house. Why were the policemen there that night? You know why they were there. Were they there to protect these Holy people from the Negroes? Oh, no. Were they there to protect the people who hate 'Eye-talians' from the Negroes? No. Were they there to protect the residents of Goethe Street? No, no, not that. Was an army to be let loose on Charlevoix and Garland? No. They were there, gentlemen, to protect the rights of a colored family who occupied the premises that they had bought. Protect them against what? Against people who would drive them out in violation of the law. Is there any doubt about that?

No, perhaps some of you gentlemen do not believe in colored men moving into white neighborhoods. Let me talk about that a minute, gentlemen. I don't want to leave any question untouched that might be important in this case, and I fancy that some of you do not believe as I believe on this question.

Let us be honest about it. There are people who buy themselves a little home and think the value of it would go down if colored people come. Perhaps it would. I don't know. I am not going to testify in this case. It may go down and it may go up. It will probably go down for some purposes and go up for others. I don't know. Suppose it does? What of it? I am sorry for anybody whose home depreciates in value. Still, you can not keep up a government for the purpose of making people's homes valuable. Noise will depreciate the value of a house, and sometimes a street car line will do it. A public school will do it. People do not like a lot of children around their house. That is one reason why they send them to school. You can not get as much for your property. Livery stables used to do it; garages do it now. Any kind of noise will do it. No man can buy a house and be sure that somebody will not depreciate its value. Something may enhance its value, of course. We are always willing to take the profit, but not willing to take the loss. Those are incidents of civilization. We get that because we refuse to live with our fellowman, that is all.

Look at the Negro's side of it. You remember Dancy. Did you ever see a brighter man than he? Compare him with Miller. Compare him with Miss S-t-o-w-e-1–1. Compare him with Andrews. Compare him with anybody on their side of this case. There isn't any comparison. Dancy is colored. He is the head of the Urban League, branch of the association of charities. His business is to look after the poor black, the ones who need it.

He told you how hard it was for colored people to find homes. Do I need to say anything about it? You, gentlemen, are here and you want to do right. Are any of you going to invite colored people to live next door to you? No. Would it hurt you? Not at all. Prejudice is so deep that it might affect the value of your property for sale purposes. Let me ask you, would not any of you like to meet Dancy? Who would you rather meet for companionship and association and fellowship, Dancy or some of the gophers up around "Goffee" Street as some call it? I know who you would rather meet.

Who would you rather meet, their white witnesses or Spalding? Now, I would put Spalding down as a real gentleman. He has some colored blood in him, but what of it? He was a student at Ann Arbor University. He has a good mind, hasn't he? Wouldn't any of you be willing to invite him into your home? I think you would. What is he doing? He is a mail carrier, because he is a black gentleman, otherwise he would have as important a position as the white man would have, with his attainments and his courtesy and his manner. He is black, partly black.

What are you, gentlemen? And what am I? I don't know. I can only go a little way toward the source of my own being. I know my father and I know my mother. I knew my great-grandmothers and my grand-fathers on both sides, but I didn't know my great grandfathers and great grand others on either side, and I don't know who they were. All that a man can do in this direction is but little. He can only slightly raise the veil that hangs over all the past. He can peer into the darkness just a little way and that is all. I know that somewhere around 1600, as the record goes, some of my ancestors came from England. Some of them I don't know where all of them came from, and I don't think any human being knows where all his ancestors came from. But back of that, I can say nothing. What do you know of yours?

I will tell you what I know, or what I think I know, gentlemen. I will try to speak as modestly as I can; knowing the uncertainty of human knowledge, because it is uncertain. The best I can do is to go a little way back. I know that back of us all and each of us is the blood of all the world. I know that it courses in your veins and in mine. It has all come out of the infinite past, and I can't pick out mine and you can't pick out yours, and it is only the ignorant who know, and I believe that back of that—back of that—is what we call the lower order of life; back of that there lurks the instinct of the distant serpent, of the carnivorous tiger. All the elements have been gathered together to make the mixture that is you and I and all the race, and nobody knows anything about his own.

Gentlemen, I wonder who we are anyhow, to be so proud about our ancestry? We had better try to do something to be proud of ourselves; we had better try to do something kindly, something humane, to some human being, than to brag about our ancestry, of which none of us know anything.

Now, let us go back to the street again. I don't know. Perhaps I weary you. Perhaps these things that seem important to me are unimportant, but they are all a part of the great human tragedy that stands before us. And if I could do something, which I can't, to make the world better, I would try to have it more tolerant, more kindly, more understanding; could I do that and nothing else, I would be glad.

The Police Department went up there on the morning of the 8th, in the City of Detroit, in the State of Michigan, U. S. A., to see that a family were permitted to move into a home that they owned without getting their throats cut by the noble Nordics who inhabit that jungle. Fine, isn't it? No race question in this? Oh, no, this is a murder case, and yet, in the forenoon of the 8th, they sent four policemen there, to protect a man and his wife with two little truck loads of household furniture who were moving into that place.

Pretty tough, isn't it? Aren't you glad you are not black? You deserve a lot of credit for it, don't you, because you didn't choose black ancestry? People ought to be killed who chose black ancestry. The policemen went there to protect the lives and the small belongings of these humble folk who moved into their home. What are these black people to do?

I seem to wander from one thing to another without much sequence. I must get back again to the colored man. You don't want him. Perhaps you don't want him next to you. Suppose you were colored. Did any of you ever dream that you were colored? Did you ever wake up out of a nightmare when you dreamed that you were colored? Would you be willing to have my client's skin. Why? Just because somebody is prejudiced!

Imagine yourselves colored, gentlemen. Imagine yourselves back in the Sweet house on that fatal night. That is the only right way to treat this case, and the court will tell you so. Would you move there? Where would you move? Dancy says there were six or seven thousand colored people here sixteen years ago. And seventy-one thousand five years ago. Gentlemen, why are they here? They came here as you came here, under the laws of trade and business, under the instincts to live; both the white and the colored, just the same; the instincts of all animals to propagate their kind, the feelings back of life and on which life depends. They came here to live. Your factories were open for them. Mr. Ford hired them. The automobile companies hired them. Everybody hired them. They were all willing to give them work, weren't they? Everyone of them.

You and I are willing to give them work, too. We are willing to have them in our houses to take care of the children and do the rough work that we shun ourselves. They are not offensive, either. We invited them; pretty nearly all the colored population has come to Detroit in the last fifteen years; most of them, anyhow. They have always had a corner on the meanest jobs. The city must grow, or you couldn't brag about it.

The colored people must live somewhere. Everybody is willing to have them live somewhere else. The people at the corner of Garland and Charlevoix would be willing to have them go to some other section. They would be willing to have them buy a place up next to Mrs. Dodge's house; but most of them haven't got money enough to do that; none that I know of. Everybody would be willing to have them go somewhere else.

Somewhere they must live. Are you going to kill them? Are you going to say that they can work, but they can't get a place to sleep? They can toil in the mill, but can't eat their dinner at home. We want them to build automobiles for us, don't we? We even let them become our chauffeurs. Oh, gentlemen, what is the use! You know it is wrong. Everyone of you know it is wrong. You know that no man in conscience could blame a Negro for almost anything. Can you think of these people without shouldering your own responsibility? Don't make it harder for them, I beg you.

They sent four policemen in the morning to help this little family move in. They had a bedstead, a stove and some bedding, ten guns and some ammunition, and they had food to last them through a siege. I feel that they should have taken less furniture and more food and guns.

Gentlemen, nature works in a queer way. I don't know how this question of color will ever be solved, or whether it will be solved. Nature has a way of doing things. There is one thing about nature, she has plenty of time. She would make broad prairies so that we can raise wheat and corn to feed men. How does she do it? She sends a glacier plowing across a continent, and takes fifty-thousand years to harrow it and make it fit to till and support human life. She makes a man. She tries endless experiments before the man is done.

She wants to make a race and it takes an infinite mixture to make it. She wants to give us some conception of human rights, and some kindness and charity and she makes pain and suffering and sorrow and death. It all counts. That is a rough way, but it is the only way. It all counts in the great, long broad scheme of things. I look on a trial like this with a feeling of disgust and shame. I can't help it now. It will be after we have learned in the terrible and expensive school of human experience that we will be willing to find each other and understand each other.

Now, let us get to the bare facts in this case. The City of Detroit had the police force there to help these people move into their home. When they unloaded their goods, men and women on the street began going from house to house. This club got busy. They went from house to house to sound the alarm, "the Negroes are coming," as if a foreign army was invading their homes; as if a wild beast had come down out of the mountains in the olden times.

I am not going over it fully. Two attractive, clever girls, who have color in their faces, without using paint, stayed at the Sweets that night, the 8th, because they did not dare go home. Can you imagine those colored people? They didn't dare move without thinking of their color. Where we go into a hotel unconsciously, or a church, if we choose, they do not. Of course, colored people belong to a church, and they have a Y. M. C. A. That is, a Jim Crow Y. M. C. A. The black Christians cannot mix with the white Christians. They will probably have a Jim Crow Heaven where the white angels will not be obliged to meet the black angels, except as servants.

These girls went out to the Sweet's house and were marooned, and did not dare to go home on account of the crowd on the streets. Was there a crowd? Schuknecht says there were more on the streets on the 8th than the 9th. Of course, I don't believe him, but he says there were more automobiles on the 9th. The papers had advertised that the colored people had come, and over on Tireman Avenue they were busy gathering the klans to help out the Nordic brother of Charlevoix and Garland.

On the 9th, what happened? I have told you something about the crowd. Are our witnesses telling the truth, or are they lying? The tire man, who is white, won't lie to help them. The newspaper man, Mr. Cohen, won't lie to help them. He went down that street just before it happened, in time to hear the sound of the stones against the Sweet house, and he told what it was and how he had to elbow his way through the crowd.

Do you believe it? Oh, no, you don't believe it. You know it, and I am wasting my time because you know it. No need to talk to a jury to correct their ideas.

That is easy. If a man has an opinion you can always change it. If he has a prejudice you can't get rid of it. It comes without reason, and is immune to reason.

I will call your attention a minute to witnesses we have brought here. Those two were white. There is another white witness. That is this motherly, attractive, Mrs. Hinteys; I don't worry about her at all. My friends of the prosecution tried to say some things about her, not so very unkindly. I don't know as I would say unkindly at all, but rather arouse suspicion in your minds as to the truth of her story. She said she didn't appear on the first trial. No, white people don't run around volunteering to be witnesses for us. She appeared in this trial, and it seems that she had done work for the mother of my associate, Thomas Chawke. When she heard that he was in the case, she went to see him and she came on this witness stand and told her story.

Now, gentlemen, you saw her. Did she tell the truth, or didn't she? Lawyers have a habit, you know, of talking about the intelligence and perfection of their own witness, and I imagine I am not breaking that habit. I have seen few people that impressed me more than Mr. and Mrs. Spalding. I have seen few young girls, no matter what their color, that impressed me more than those two girls who spent the night in that house. I was impressed with Smith's story. It was obviously true. He had such difficulty getting through Garland Street that night. His car was stoned because his face was black. Everybody knows that the automobile man would have no reason for lying, and that if he could choose to do anything, he would testify on the other side. I don't need to suggest to anybody that the newspaper man was telling the truth. And if he tells the truth, it settles this case.

Is the old lady telling the truth? She is the kind we don't see as much of now as we once did see. She is the working woman. Of course, you don't see them very much except when you come in the house and visit the kitchen. But I am older than most of you, I guess,—than any of you. Anyway, I have seen them. A woman with a fine face. She probably would have called that "Goethy" Street, like the rest, because she hasn't much education. She isn't like the rest of the mob. A fine, honest face. She knew exactly what she was talking about and she told the truth. As I looked at her on the witness stand, it seemed to me that I could see through her face; her face covered with the scars of life, and fight, and hard work, to the inward beauty that shone through it. I could almost feel the years slipping away from me and leaving me a boy again in the simple country town where I was born; I could see my mother and her companions who swept their own houses, did their own washing and baked their own bread and made clothes for the children; they were kind, simple, human and honest.

There isn't a man on this jury who could be persuaded to believe that this woman wasn't honest. She said there were five hundred people on the corner alone. Is there any doubt about that? She said "more than five hundred." She said "twice as many as there are in this room."

Now let's see what Schuknecht said, and then I shall skip a little. I know you wish I would skip a lot more. There were certain things that did happen that night, weren't there? There was a crowd there. They began coming as the dusk gathered.

They don't work in the daylight; not those fellows. They are too good for daylight work. They came as the dusk gathered. They came in taxis and automobiles and on foot. They came on every street that centered at Charlevoix; they came down the sidewalk and over across the street, where they gathered in that school yard; the school yard, gentlemen, of all the places on earth; the schoolyard where they made their deadly assault upon justice and honesty and law, and they were gathered there five hundred strong. Still this was no doubt the only occasion that most of them had ever needed a schoolhouse.

Schuknecht stood out in front, didn't he? He had this in charge. I don't need to go beyond the witnesses who appeared here for the State. He stood there on that corner, in front of the schoolhouse. His brother-in-law came up twice or three times to see him. Do you remember him? He worked for the telegraph company. Why did he come? "Looking for my boy." Yes, he was looking for his boy. He came up, and he asked nobody about the boy, and he went back to his home, still looking for his boy, and came back looking for his boy again, and went back once more and came back again looking for his boy.

Now, I am just a little doubtful in my mind whether he is telling the truth or not. I will give you two theories, and you can choose. He either said that he was looking for his boy so he could claim that he was not there, looking for the riot that he knew was coming; or he knew what was coming and he was afraid for the life of his boy and was hunting him. Take your choice. I have thought of both ideas. Sometimes I take one view and sometimes another! But, anyway, he was there looking for his boy. "Where is my wandering boy tonight?" was the song he seemed to be singing, right around that corner. Poor boy. You have been away from home before. It was only dusk. "My God, I must find that boy."

Well, gentlemen, strange, isn't it, and up there above the Sweet house, coming down, on the other side of the street was a woman, Abbie, looking for her girl, nineteen years old. Mr. Toms thinks she was too old to disturb her mother, but I will tell you this, if a mother lived to be one hundred and she had a girl, seventy-five, she would still be looking for her. She was looking for a girl wandering up and down the street, in front of the Sweet house; a strange place to be looking for a girl. She might have gone in there and got eaten by the blacks. In front of the Sweet house, of all the places in the world, and then she went back, and then she went across to the Dove house, and didn't see anybody there, but Breiner got shot, and we left her looking for her girl.

And on this corner was that devoted husband, the most devoted husband I ever heard of, in court, at least. I have read about them in fairy-stories; fairy-stories and cheap novels. I have read about devoted wives, and I have read about devoted husbands, but this husband pacing back and forth for almost an hour watching for his wife to get off the car at the corner in front of her house certainly takes the cake. Maybe he really loved his wife; I don't know. Such things have happened, and maybe he didn't know just when this show was going to begin, gentlemen. Maybe he was worried, and on the other side of the street was a lady looking for her girl.

All the fathers and all the mothers and all the husbands and all the wives were gathering the chickens under their wings for the coming storm. Weren't they? Just before eight o'clock. They were clearing the decks for action and getting the children out of the schoolyard and out of the crowd, so that the only strong, healthy men, and plenty of them, could get these "gun" men who were trying to live in their own home.

What was Schuknecht doing? Now, gentlemen, let us see about that again. I never say much about policemen.

Mr. Toms:	What was that?
Mr. Darrow:	I never say much about policemen. Do I?
Mr. Toms:	That is what you said, but I couldn't believe it.
Mr. Darrow:	I am going to be very easy on Schuknecht. I have often seen good policemen. I mean, good men who were policemen. But, now, Schuknecht said that he had this matter in his charge. Didn't he? He stood right there on the corner. He did wander a little bit, but not much; inside of the block all the time, knowing that the whole responsibility rested on him. He had eight men early in that evening besides himself; and another officer. That made ten; and then as the night wore on, and the darkness began to gather, the darkness and the crowd came down together on those four corners.

They sent for two more policemen. Then they put policemen on the four corners a block away and blocked the street. For what? There wasn't any crowd there. Nobody says it was a crowd, unless they are lying; just a "few;" a "few;" and they blocked the streets. Gentlemen, none of you look like you were born yesterday. Maybe you were; I can not tell. And then a little later, what happened? They sent for two more policemen. At the station they had twenty or thirty in reserve waiting for a riot call. Didn't they? They had ten or twelve policemen, twenty or thirty waiting for a riot call, and they sent up for two more, in a hurry, and they hustled down.

And then two policemen were sent to the top of that flat across the way, where they could "view the landscape" o'er the highest point of vantage, which, of course, would be used to protect the civilization and culture of Charlevoix Avenue; and they had just got started to go to the top of the flat when they sent for six more.

Gentlemen, six more policemen, making some fifteen or eighteen policemen around that corner. Was there any need of it? It was perfectly peaceful. Only four people on the schoolhouse grounds, according to some of them. Nothing doing. All quiet on the Potomac; warm summer evening, and the children lying on the lawn. Children, gentlemen,—children. There might have been some children earlier in the evening, but they had all been gathered under their mothers' wings before that time, and most of the women had disappeared. Just before these fatal shots were fired. Why were the policemen there?

Gentlemen, do we need anything else? If we need anything else, it is this: If we need anything else to show the hostility of the crowd that was there, it is this: A policeman swore that one window that we claim was broken at the time was really broken afterwards. Why? Who would take a "pebble" to break the windows out of these poor peoples' home after they were safely lodged in jail? And the policemen were in charge. This shooting was on the 9th of September; six or seven months have passed away since then; all these defendants were in jail two or three months, and since that they have been out on bail, but a policeman still stands guard on that vacant home to protect it from being destroyed by the people who want to have an American community where they can raise their families "in peace and amity."

Gentlemen, supposing you return a verdict of not guilty in this case, which you will; I would be ashamed to think you would not; what would happen if this man and his wife and his child, moved into that house? They have the same right to go to that house that you have to your home, after your services are done. What will happen? Don't you know? What did Schuknecht say? Eight or ten policemen were standing around that house for two days and two nights. A menacing crowd was around them, wasn't there? The police were protecting them. Did one policeman ever go to one person in that crowd and say: "What are you here for?"

There was a mob assembled there. The Court will tell you what a mob is. I don't need to tell you. He will tell you that three or more people gathered together with a hostile intent is a mob; there were five hundred; they were plotting against the persons of these people and their lives, perhaps, as well. Did any policeman try to disperse it? Did they raise their hands or their voices, or do one single thing? Did they step up to any man and say: "Why are you here?" Never. They stood around there or sat around there like bumps on a log, while the mob was violating the Constitution and the laws of the State, and offending every instinct of justice and mercy and humanity.

Schuknecht was standing there; five or six others were standing there, weren't they, gentlemen? Let us see how closely they were guarding the house. They did nothing. They heard no stones thrown against that house; not one of them; and yet they were not twenty feet away. The State brought here some twenty stones gathered next morning from the house and yard, and nobody knows how many more there were. Gentlemen, a roof slopes at an incline of forty-five degrees, or about that. You can get the exact figures if you want them. Imagine some one throwing stones against the roof. How many of them would stay there, or how many of them would stay in the immediate yard, and how many of them would be left there after the mob had finished and sought to protect itself, and the police and crowd had gathered them up, the police force which was responsible for this tragedy? None of them heard a stone, and yet they were there to protect that home. None of them heard the broken glass, but they were there to protect that home. None of them saw two men come in a taxi, except one who hesitated and finally admitted that it seemed as if he did; but none of the rest. Gentlemen, you could have looted that house and moved it away and the police would never have known it. That is the way these people were protected.

[Break for lunch.]

I was speaking before luncheon about the people around the house, and the wonderful protection the blacks had. Nobody can tell exactly how many were there, of course. Here is a man, a real estate dealer, who had an office at the corner of St. Clair and Charlevoix, just a block away. He came down that night,—he was in the habit of staying at his office, and he had a partner. Real estate men are pretty wary people, you know. They don't miss many chances. If there is anybody around that looks like a prospect, they are on hand. He came down and saw that crowd. What did he do? He went over to this apartment-building on the corner. He stuck around the apartment-building ten or fifteen minutes or half an hour, I don't know just how long, and he leaves his office open. He stuck around ten or fifteen minutes and then went back to his office; not to make a sale, but to get his partner, who was the only man in charge of the office. And so the two of them started back and stood there on the corner until the shooting began.

What do you suppose they were there for? Real estate men don't waste time with a crowd around the office. Not only was he content and brought his partner, and left nobody in the office. He didn't even stop to lock the door, and they stayed there on the corner until the shooting began.

Witnesses forget themselves and tell the truth. Why were the police telling people to move on? All the witnesses said they were not permitted to stand near the house. Why do they, every once in a while, pull themselves up and say that the crowd was so and so? Why does the little boy come into this court room and on the first trial of this case say: "I saw a large crowd," and then pull himself up; "I saw a great many people," and then say, "I saw a few?" And then on cross-examination admit that he had been told to do it, and had forgot himself when he said a great many people? This is in the record as coming from the last case, and he said it was true. It was true, and every man in this case who has listened to it knows that it is true.

Oh, they say, there is nothing to justify this shooting; it was an orderly, neighborly crowd; an orderly, neighborly crowd. They came there for a purpose and intended to carry it out. How long, pray, would these men wait penned up in that house? How long would you wait? The very presence of the crowd was a mob, as I believe the Court will tell you.

Suppose a crowd gathers around your house; a crowd which doesn't want you there; a hostile crowd, for a part of two days and two nights, until the police force of the city is called in to protect you. How long, tell me, are you going to live in that condition with a mob surrounding your house and the police force standing in front of it? How long should these men have waited? I can imagine why they waited as long as they did. You wouldn't have waited. Counsel say they had just as good reason to shoot on the 8th as on the 9th. Concede it. They did not shoot. They waited and hoped and prayed that in some way this crowd would pass them by and grant them the right to live.

The mob came back the next night and the colored people waited while they were gathering; they waited while they were coming from every street and every corner, and while the officers were supine and helpless and doing nothing. And they waited until dozens of stones were thrown against the house on the roof, probably—don't know how many. Nobody knows how many. They waited until the windows were broken before they shot. Why did they wait so long? I think I know.

How much chance had these people for their life after they shot; surrounded by a crowd, as they were? They would never take a chance unless they thought it was necessary to take the chance. Eleven black people penned up in the face of a mob. What chance did they have?

Suppose they shot before they should. What is the theory of counsel in this case? Nobody pretends there is anything in this case to prove that our client Henry fired the fatal shot. There isn't the slightest. It wasn't a shot that would fit the gun he had. The theory of this case is that he was a part of a combination to do something. Now, what was that combination, gentlemen? Your own sense will tell you what it was. Did they combine to go there and kill somebody? Were they looking for somebody to murder?

Dr. Sweet scraped together his small earnings by his industry and put himself through college, and he scraped together his small earnings of three thousand dollars to buy that home because he wanted to kill somebody? It is silly to talk about it. He bought that home just as you buy yours, because he wanted a home to live in, to take his wife and to raise his family. There is no difference between the love of a black man for his offspring and the love of a white. He and his wife had the same feeling of fatherly and motherly affection for their child that you gentlemen have for yours, and that your father and mother had for you. They bought that home for that purpose; not to kill somebody.

They might have feared trouble, as they probably did, and as the evidence shows that every man with a black face fears it, when he moved into a home that is fit for a dog to live in. It is part of the curse that, for some inscrutable reason, has followed the race—if you call it a race—and which curse, let us hope, sometime the world will be wise enough and decent enough and human enough to wipe out.

They went there to live. They knew the dangers. Why do you suppose they took these guns and this ammunition and these men there? Because they wanted to kill somebody? It is utterly absurd and crazy. They took them there because they thought it might be necessary to defend their home with their lives and they were determined to do it. They took guns there that in case of need they might fight, fight even to death for their home, and for each other, for their people, for their race, for their rights under the Constitution and the laws under which all of us live; and unless men and women will do that, we will soon be a race of slaves, whether we are black or white. "Eternal vigilance is the price of liberty," and it has always been so and always will be. Do you suppose they were in there for any other purpose? Gentlemen, there isn't a chance that they took arms there for anything else.

They did go there knowing their rights, feeling their responsibility, and determined to maintain those rights if it meant death to the last man and the last woman, and no one could do more. No man lived a better life or died a better death than fighting for his home and his children, for himself, and for the eternal principles upon which life depends. Instead of being here under indictment, for murder, they should be honored for the brave stand they made, for their rights and ours. Some day, both white and black, irrespective of color, will honor the memory of these men, whether they are inside prison walls or outside, and will recognize that they fought not only for themselves, but for every man who wishes to be free.

Did they shoot too quick? Tell me just how long a man needs wait for a mob? The Court, I know, will instruct you on that. How long do you need to wait for a mob?

We have been told that because a person trespasses on your home or on your ground you have no right to shoot him. Is that true? If I go up to your home in a peaceable way, and go on your ground, or on your porch, you have no right to shoot me. You have a right to use force to put me off if I refuse to go, even to the extent of killing me. That isn't this case, gentlemen. That isn't the case of a neighbor who went up to the yard of a neighbor without permission and was shot to death. Oh, no. The Court will tell you the difference, unless I am mistaken, and I am sure I am not; unless I mistake the law, and I am sure, I do not.

This isn't a case of a man who trespasses upon the ground of some other man and is killed. It is the case of an unlawful mob, which in itself is a crime; a mob bent on mischief; a mob that has no rights. They are too dangerous. It is like a fire. One man may do something. Two will do a much more; three will do more than three times as much; a crowd will do something that no man ever dreamed of doing. The law recognizes it. It is the duty of every man—I don't care who he is, to disperse a mob. It is the duty of the officers to disperse them. It was the duty of the inmates of the house, even though they had to kill somebody to do it. Now, gentlemen, I wouldn't ask you to take the law on my statement. The Court will tell you the law. A mob is a criminal combination of itself. Their presence is enough. You need not wait until it spreads. It is there, and that is enough. There is no other law; there hasn't been for years, and it is the law which will govern this case.

Now, gentlemen, how long did they need to wait? Why, it is silly. How long would you wait? How long do you suppose ten white men would be waiting? Would they have waited as long? I will tell you how long they needed to wait. I will tell you what the law is, and the Court will confirm me, I am sure. Every man may act upon appearances as they seem to him. Every man may protect his own life. Every man has the right to protect his own property. Every man is bound under the law to disperse a mob even to the extent of taking life. It is his duty to do it, but back of that he has the human right to go to the extent of killing to defend his life. He has a right to defend the life of his kinsman, servant, his friends, or those about him, and he has a right to defend, gentlemen, not from real danger, but from what seems to him real danger at the time.

Here is Henry Sweet, the defendant in this case, a boy. How many of you know why you are trying him? What had he to do with it? Why is he in this case? A boy, twenty-one years old, working his way through college, and he is just as good a boy as the boy of any juror in this box; just as good a boy as you people were when you were boys, and I submit to you, he did nothing whatever that was wrong.

Of course, we lawyers talk and talk and talk, as if we feared results. I don't mean to trifle with you. I always fear results. When life or liberty is in the hands of a lawyer, he realizes the terrible responsibility that is on him, and he fears that some word will be left unspoken, or some thought will be forgotten. I would not be telling you the truth if I told you that I did not fear the result of this important case; and when my judgment and my reason comes to my aid and takes counsel with my fears, I know, and I feel perfectly well that no twelve American jurors, especially in any northern land, could be brought together who would dream of taking a boy's life or liberty under circumstances like this. That is what my judgment tells me, but my fears perhaps cause me to go further and to say more when I should not have said as much.

Now, let me tell you when a man has the right to shoot in self-defense, and in defense of his home; not when these vital things in life are in danger, but when he thinks they are. These despised blacks did not need to wait until the house was beaten down above their heads. They didn't need to wait until every window was broken. They didn't need to wait longer for that mob to grow more inflamed. There is nothing so dangerous as ignorance and bigotry when it is unleashed as it was here. The Court will tell you that these inmates of this house had the right to decide upon appearances, and if they did, even though they were mistaken they are not guilty. I don't know but they could safely have stayed a little longer. I don't know but it would have been well enough to let this mob break a few more windowpanes. I don't know but it would have been better and been safe to have let them batter down the house before they shot. I don't know.

How am I to tell, and how are you to tell? You are twelve white men, gentlemen. You are twelve men sitting here eight months after all this occurred, listening to the evidence, perjured and otherwise, in this court, to tell whether they acted too quickly or too slowly. A man may be running an engine out on the railroad. He may stop too quickly or too slowly. In an emergency he is bound to do one or the other, and the jury a year after, sitting in cold blood, may listen to the evidence and say that he acted too quickly. What do they know about it? You must sit out there upon a moving engine with your hand on the throttle and facing danger and must decide and act quickly. Then you can tell.

Cases often occur in the courts, which doesn't speak very well for the decency of courts, but they have happened, where men have been shipwrecked at sea, a number of the men having left the ship and gone into a small boat to save their lives; they have floated around for hours and tossed on the wild waves of an angry sea; their food disappearing, the boat heavy and likely to sink and no friendly sail in sight,—What are they to do? Will they throw some of their companions off the boat and save the rest? Will they eat some to save the others? If they kill anybody, it is because they want to live. Every living thing wants to live. The strongest instinct in life is to keep going. You have seen a tree upon a rock send a shoot down for ten or fifteen or twenty feet, to search for water, to draw it up, that it may still survive; it is a strong instinct with animals and with plants, with all sentient things, to keep alive.

Men are out in a boat, in an angry sea, with little food, and less water. No hope in sight. What will they do? They throw a companion overboard to save themselves, or they kill somebody to save themselves. Juries have come into court and passed on the question of whether they should have waited longer, or not. Later, the survivors were picked up by a ship and perhaps, if they had waited longer, all would have been saved; yet a jury, months after it was over, sitting safely in their jury-box, pass upon the question of whether they acted too quickly or not.

Can they tell? No. To decide that case, you must be in a small boat, with little food and water; in a wild sea, with no sail in sight, and drifting around for hours or days in the face of the deep, beset by hunger and darkness and fear and hope. Then you can tell; but, no man can tell without it. It can't be done, gentlemen, and the law says so, and this Court will tell you so.

Let me tell you what you must do, gentlemen. It is fine for lawyers to say, naively, that nothing happened. No foot was set upon that ground; as if you had to put your foot on the premises. You might put your hand on. The foot isn't sacred. No foot was set upon their home. No shot was fired, nothing except that the house was stoned and windows broken; and an angry crowd was outside seeking their destruction. That is all. That is all, gentlemen. I say that no American citizen, unless he is black, need wait until an angry mob sets foot upon his premises before he kills. I say that no free man need wait to see just how far an aggressor will go before he takes life.

The first instinct a man has is to save his life. He doesn't need to experiment. He hasn't time to experiment. When he thinks it is time to save his life, he has the right to act. There isn't any question about it. It has been the law of every English speaking country so long as we have had law. Every man's home is his castle, which even the King may not enter. Every man has a right to kill to defend himself or his family, or others, either in the defense of the home or in the defense of themselves.

So far as that branch of the case is concerned, there is only one thing that this jury has a right to consider, and that is whether the defendants acted in honest fear of danger. That is all. Perhaps they could have safely waited longer. I know a little about psychology. If I could talk to a man long enough, and not too long, and he talk to me a little, I could guess fairly well what is going on in his head, but I can't understand the psychology of a mob, and neither can anybody else. We know it is unreasoning. We know it is filled with hatred. We know it is cruel. We know it has no heart, no soul, and no pity. We know it is as cruel as the grave. No man has a right to stop and dicker while waiting for a mob.

Now, let us look at these fellows. Here were eleven colored men, penned up in the house. Put yourselves in their place. Make yourselves colored for a little while. It won't hurt, you can wash it off. They can't, but you can; just make yourself black men for a little while; long enough, gentlemen, to judge them, and before any of you would want to be judged, you would want your juror to put himself in your place. That is all I ask in this case, gentlemen. They were black, and they knew the history of the black.

Our friend makes fun of Dr. Sweet and Henry Sweet talking these things all over in the short space of two months. Well, gentlemen, let me tell you something, that isn't evidence. This is just theory. This is just theory, and nothing else. I should imagine that the only thing that two or three colored people talk of when they get together is race. I imagine that they can't rub color off their face or rub it out of their minds. I imagine that is it with them always. I imagine that the stories of lynchings, the stories of murders, the stories of oppression is a topic of constant conversation. I imagine that everything that appears in the newspapers on this subject is carried from one to another until every man knows what others know, upon the topic which is the most important of all to their lives.

What do you think about it? Suppose you were black. Do you think you would forget it even in your dreams? Or would you have black dreams? Suppose you had to watch every point of contact with your neighbor and remember your color, and you knew your children were growing up under this handicap. Do you suppose you would think of anything else?

Well, gentlemen, I imagine that a colored man would think of that before he would think of where he could get bootleg whiskey, even. Do you suppose this boy coming in here didn't know all about the conditions, and did not learn all about them? Did he not know about Detroit? Do you suppose he hadn't read the story of his race? He is intelligent. He goes to school. He would have been a graduate now, except for this long hesitation, when he is waiting to see whether he goes back to college or goes to jail. Do you suppose that black students and teachers are discussing it?

Anyhow, gentlemen, what is the use? The jury isn't supposed to be entirely ignorant. They are supposed to know something. These black people were in the house with the black man's psychology, and with the black man's fear, based, on what they had heard and what they had read and what they knew. I don't need to go far. I don't need to travel to Florida. I don't even need to talk about the Chicago riots. The testimony showed that in Chicago a colored boy on a raft had been washed to a white bathing beach, and men and boys of my race stoned him to death. A riot began, and some hundred and twenty were killed.

I don't need to go to Washington or to St. Louis. Let us take Detroit. I don't need to go far either in space or time. Let us take this city. Now, gentlemen, I am not saying that the white people of Detroit are different from the white people of any other city. I know what has been done in Chicago. I know what prejudice growing out of race and religion has done the world over, and all through time. I am not blaming Detroit. I am stating what has happened, that is all. And I appeal to you, gentlemen, to do your part to save the honor of this city, to save its reputation, to save yours, to save its name, and to save the poor colored people who can not save themselves.

I was told there had not been a lynching of a colored man in thirty years or more in Michigan. All right. Why, I can remember when the early statesmen of Michigan cared for the colored man and when they embodied the rights of the colored men in the constitution and statutes. I can remember when they laid the foundation that made it possible for a man of any color or any religion, or any creed, to own his home wherever he could find a man to sell it. I remember when civil rights laws were passed that gave the Negro the right to go where the white man went and as he went. There are some men who seem to think those laws were wrong. I do not. Wrong or not, it is the law, and if you were black you would protest with every fiber of your body your right to live.

Michigan used to protect the rights of colored people. There were not many of them here, but they have come in the last few years, and with them has come prejudice. Then, too, the southern white man has followed his black slave. But that isn't all. Black labor has come in competition with white. Prejudices have been created where there was no prejudice before. We have listened to the siren song that we are a superior race and have superior rights, and that the black man has none.

It is a new idea in Detroit that a colored man's home can be torn down about his head because he is black. There are some eighty thousand blacks here now, and they are bound to reach out. They have reached out in the past, and they will reach out in the future. Do not make any mistake, gentlemen. I am making no promises. I know the instinct for life. I know it reaches black and white alike. I know that you can not confine any body of people to any particular place, and, as the population grows, the colored people will go farther. I know it, and you must change the law or you must take it as it is, or you must invoke the primal law of nature and get back to clubs and fists, and if you are ready for that, gentlemen, all right, but do it with your eyes open. That is all I care for. You must have a government of law or blind force, and if you are ready to let blind force take the place of law, the responsibility is on you, not on me.

Now, let us see what has happened here. So far as I know, there had been nothing of the sort happened when Dr. Sweet bought his home. He took an option on it in May, and got his deed in June; and in July, in that one month, while he was deliberating on moving, there were three cases of driving Negro families out of their homes in Detroit. This was accomplished by stones, clubs, guns and mobs.

Suppose one of you were colored and had bought a house on Garland Avenue. Take this just exactly as it is. You bought it in June, intending to move in July, and you read and heard about what happened to Dr. Turner in another part of the city. Would you have waited? Would you have waited a month, as Sweet did? Suppose you had heard of what happened to Bristol? Would you have waited? Remember, these men didn't have any too much money. Dr. Sweet paid three thousand dollars on his home, leaving a loan on it of sixteen thousand dollars more. He had to scrape together some money to buy his furniture, and he bought fourteen hundred dollars worth the day after he moved in and paid two hundred dollars down.

Gentlemen, it is only right to consider Dr. Sweet and his family. He has a little child. He has a wife. They must live somewhere. If they could not, it would be better to take them out and kill them, and kill them decently and quickly. Had he any right to be free?

They determined to move in and to take nine men with them. What would you have done, gentlemen? If you had courage, you would have done as Dr. Sweet did. You would have been crazy or a coward if you hadn't. Would you have moved in alone? No, you would not have gone alone. You would have taken your wife. If you had a brother or two, you would have taken them because you would know, that you could rely on them, and you would have taken those nearest to you. And you would have moved in just as Dr. Sweet did. Wouldn't you? He didn't shoot the first night. He didn't look for trouble. He kept his house dark so that the neighbors wouldn't see him. He didn't dare have a light in his house, gentlemen, for fear of the neighbors. Noble neighbors, who were to have a colored family in their neighborhood. He had the light put out in the front part of the house, so as not to tempt any of the mob to violence.

Now, let us go back a little. What happened before this? I don't need to go over the history of the case. Everybody who wants to understand knows it, and many who don't want to understand it. As soon as Dr. Sweet bought this house, the neighbors organized the "Water Works Park Improvement Association." They made a constitution and by-laws. You may read the constitution and by-laws of every club, whether it is the Rotary Club or the—I was trying to think of some other club, but I can't. Whatever the club, it must always have a constitution and by-laws. These are all about the same. You cannot tell anything about a man by the church he belongs to. You can't tell anything about him by the kind of clothes he wears. You can't tell anything about him by any of these extraneous matters, and you can't tell anything about an association from the by-laws. Not a thing. I belonged to associations in my time. As far as I can remember, they all had by-laws.

Mr. Toms: All of them have the same by-laws?

Mr. Darrow: Yes, all have the same. They are all of them engaged in the work of uplifting humanity, and humanity still wants to stay down. All engaged in the same work, according to their by-laws, gentlemen. So, the "Water Works Park Improvement Club" had by-laws. They were going to aid the police. They didn't get a chance to try to aid them until that night. They were going to regulate automobile traffic. They didn't get any chance to regulate automobile traffic until that night. They were going to protect the homes and make them safe for children.

The purpose was clear, and every single member reluctantly said that they joined it to keep colored people out of the district. They might have said it first as well as last. People, even in a wealthy and aristocratic neighborhood like Garland and Charlevoix, don't give up a dollar without expecting some profit; not a whole dollar. Sometimes two in one family, the husband and wife, joined.

They got in quick. The woods were on fire. Something had to be done, as quick as they heard that Dr. Sweet was coming; Dr. Sweet, who had been a bellhop on a boat, and a bellhop in hotels, and fired furnaces and sold popcorn and has worked his way with his great handicap through school and through college, and graduated as a doctor, and gone to Europe and taken another degree; Dr. Sweet, who knew more than any man in the neighborhood ever would know or ever want to know. He deserved more for all he had done. When they heard he was coming, then it was time to act, and act together, for the sake of their homes, their families and their firesides, and so they got together. They didn't wait. A meeting was called in the neighborhood; we haven't a record of that, but we have a record of another one.

And then, what happened after that? Let me read you, not from the books of any organization; not from colored people; from what I have learned is a perfectly respectable paper, so far as papers go, the Detroit Free Press.

Mr. Toms: Free Press, the best morning paper.

Mr. Darrow: And the only real Free Press that I ever heard of. On July 12th, gentlemen, a month after Dr. Sweet had bought his home, this appears in the paper, the headlines: "Stop Rioting." "Smith Pleads with Citizens. Detroit Faces Shame and Disgrace as the Result of Fighting, he states." "Negro, held for shooting youth, vacates residence under police guard."

Here is the story, not published in colored papers:

"While Detroit police were anticipating further outbreaks near the homes occupied by Negroes in white residential areas and had full complements of reserves in readiness to deal with any situation that might arise, Mayor John W. Smith late yesterday issued a statement asking the public to see that the riots 'do not grow into a condition which will be a lasting stain on the reputation of Detroit as a law-abiding community.'

"The storm centers are considered to be American and Tireman Avenues [*in southwestern Detroit: ed.*] where Vollington A. Bristol, Negro undertaker . . ."

Excuse me. This isn't the only time I ever heard of that Tireman Avenue.

"The storm centers are considered to be American and Tireman Avenues where Vollington A. Bristol, Negro undertaker still occupies the home he recently purchased there in the teeth of demonstrations on three successive nights and a residence on Prairie Avenue, near Grand River Avenue."

"John W. Fletcher, 9428 Stoepel Avenue, two blocks from Livernois and Plymouth Avenue, the Negro who is to be charged with causing grievous bodily harm in connection with the shooting of a white youth, Leonard Paul, 15 years old, 9567 Prairie Avenue, Friday night, relieved the situation in his district by moving out yesterday after less than forty-eight hours tenancy. Six patrolmen, under Lieutenant A. R. Saal of the Petosky Avenue Station, were at hand as Fletcher moved his furniture over his brick-strewn lawn from the house in which not one window remained whole."

Gentlemen, what kind of feeling does it give a white man? It makes me ashamed of my race. Now, to go on:

"There was no trouble.

"Latest reports from Receiving Hospital indicates that the youth, Paul, who was twice shot in the hip by Fletcher, according to the latter's alleged statement, is still in a serious condition.

"Although no demonstrations were held up to a late hour last night, police guards will be maintained for an indefinite period about the three homes, it was announced. Two of the houses have been purchased and occupied by Negro families, and negotiations are under way for the purchase of the third by a Negro, according to rumors which have reached the police. The latter is on Prairie Avenue.

"The police armored car, which was conditioned early last week and has been held in readiness in case of trouble, last night was moved near the scene of the recent disturbances. It will remain for the present in the vicinity of Tireman and American Avenues. Every available policeman and detective, and fifty deputy sheriffs also have been detailed to the locality.

"A meeting, attended by more than ten thousand persons, was held on West Fourth Street, a mile west of Lincoln Park Village last night. A speaker from Tennessee advocated laws to compel Negroes to live only in certain quarters of the city."

I don't know whether he was one of the policemen who was up at the Sweet house. This speaker was from Tennessee.

"The only incident noted occurred when Bristol left this house. As he greeted Sergeant Welsh and two officers who stood on guard, an automobile passed by and swerved towards the pavement where the Negro was. The latter jumped back hurriedly, and the car kept on its way."

Mayor Smith's statement is as follows:

"Recent incidents of violence and attempted violence in connection with racial disagreements constitute a warning to the people of Detroit which they cannot afford to ignore. They are to be deplored, and it is a duty which rests as much upon the citizenry as upon the public officials to see that they do not grow into a condition which will be a lasting stain upon the reputation of Detroit as a law-abiding community."

"The police department can have but one duty in connection with all such incidents,—that is, to use its utmost endeavors to prevent the destruction of life and property. In the performance of this duty, I trust that every police officer will be unremitting in his efforts. The law recognizes no distinction in color or race. On all occasions when the emotions are deeply stirred by controversy, the persons affected on all sides of the dispute are likely to feel that the police or other controlling force are siding against them. I hope and believe that the police during the recent attempts to preserve law and order have done so impartially.

"With the police department doing its utmost to preserve order, there is always the possibility that uncontrolled elements may reach such proportions that even these efforts will not be completely effectual. It is that fact that calls for earnest cooperation by all good citizens at this time. Curiosity seekers who go to scenes of threatened disorder add immeasurably to the problem of preserving order.

Thus, the persons innocent of ill intentions are likely to be chiefly responsible for inexcusable incidents."

"The condition which faces Detroit is one which faced Washington, East St. Louis, Chicago and other large cities. The result in those cities was one which Detroit must avoid, if possible. A single fatal riot would injure this city beyond remedy."

"The avoidance of further disorder belongs to the good sense of the leaders of thought in both white and colored races. The persons either white or colored who attempt to urge their fellows on to disorder and crime are guilty of the most serious offense upon the statute books. It is clear that a thoughtless individual of both races constitutes the nucleus in each disorder, and it is equally clear that the inspiration for their acts comes from malign influences which are willing to go even to the limits of bloodshed to gain their ends. The police are expected to inquire and prosecute any persons active in organizing such disorder or inciting a riot. The rest of the duty for preserving order lies with the individual citizens—by refraining from adding to the crowds in districts where danger exists, from refraining from discussion which may have a tendency to incite disorder, and finally to rebuke at once the individual agitators who are willing to risk human life, destroy property, and ruin their city's reputation."

That is the Mayor's proclamation. The newspaper adds this:

"To maintain the high standard of the residential district between Jefferson and Mack Avenues, a meeting has been called by the Water Works Improvement Association for Thursday night in the Howe School auditorium. Men and women of the district, which includes Cadillac, Hurlburt, Bewick, Garland, St. Clair, and Harding Avenues, are asked to "attend in self-defense."

I shall not talk to you much longer. I am sorry I have talked so long. But this case is close to my heart. These colored people read this story in the paper. Do I need to go anywhere else to find the feeling of peril over the question of color? Dr. Sweet had to face the same proposition. Two nights after this story was in the paper, at the Howe School, across the street from Dr. Sweet's house, seven hundred people of the neighborhood were present; two detectives, and all the neighbors, and in their presence, a man from Tireman Avenue, who they say was radical, and who, this good gentleman, Mr. Andrews, says, called a spade a spade. Well, well, what do you know about that? He called a spade a spade. I suppose Andrews meant that he called a black man a "nigger," and "said that where the nigger showed his head, the white must shoot." He advocated force and violence. He told what had happened in his own neighborhood. He told of driving people out of their homes, and said that the Tireman Avenue Improvement Association could be called on to help at Garland and Charlevoix.

Gentlemen, we know the work of an improvement association. If you can only get enough improvement associations in the City of Detroit, Detroit will be improved. This meeting occurred July the 14th, and Sweet moved into the house September 8th. The people knew it. They were confronted with the mob. Their house was stoned. Their windows were broken. No more riotous combination ever came together than the one that was there assembled.

Who are these people who were in this house? Were they people of character? Were they people of standing? Were they people of intelligence?

First, there was Doctor Sweet. Gentlemen, a white man does pretty well when he does what Doctor Sweet did. A white boy who can start in with nothing, and put himself through college, study medicine, taking post graduate work in Europe, earning every penny of it as he goes along, shoveling snow and coal, and working as a bell hop, on boats, working at every kind of employment that he can get to make his way, is some fellow.

But, Dr. Sweet has the handicap of the color of his face. And there is no handicap more terrible than that. Supposing you had your choice, right here this minute, would you rather lose your eyesight or become colored? Would you rather lose your hearing or be a Negro? Would you rather go out there on the street and have your leg cut off by a street car, or have a black skin?

I don't like to speak of it; I do not like to speak of it in the presence of these colored people, whom I have always urged to be as happy as they can. But, it is true, Life is a hard game, anyhow. But, when the cards are stacked against you, it is terribly hard. And they are stacked against a race for no reason but that they are black.

Who are these men who were in this house? There was Doctor Sweet. There was his brother, who was a dentist. There was this young boy who worked his way for three years through college, with a little aid from his brother, and who was on his way to graduate. Henry's future is now in your hands. There was his companion, who was working his way through college,—all gathered in that house.

Were they hoodlums? Were they criminals? Were they anything except men who asked for a chance to live; who asked for a chance to breathe the free air and make their own way, earn their own living, and get their bread by the sweat of their brow?

I will read to you what the Mayor said. I will call your attention to one sentence in it again, and then let us see what the mob did. This was the Mayor of your City, whose voice should be heard, who speaks of the danger that is imminent to this city and to every other city in the north, a danger that may bear fruit at any time; and he called the attention of the public of this city to this great danger, gentlemen. And, I want to call your attention to it. Here is what he said:

> "The avoidance of further disorder belongs to the good sense of the leaders of thought of both white and colored races. The persons, either white or colored, who attempt to urge their fellows to disorder and crime, are guilty of the most serious offences upon the statute books."

Gentlemen, were those words of wisdom? Are they true? They were printed in this newspaper on the 12th day of July. Two days later, on the schoolhouse grounds, a crowd of seven or eight hundred assembled, and listened to a firebrand who arose in that audience and told the people that his community had driven men and women from their homes because they were black; that the Tireman Avenue people knew how to deal with them, and advised the mob to violate the law and the constitution and the rights of the black; advised them to take the law into their own hands, and to drive these poor dependent people from their own homes. And, the crowd cheered; while the officers of the law were there, all within two days of the time the Mayor of this city had called the attention of the public to the fact that any man was a criminal of the worst type who would do anything to stir up sedition or disobedience to the law in relation to color.

The man is more than a firebrand who invited and urged crime and violence in his community. No officer raised his hand to prosecute, and no citizen raised his voice, while this man uttered those treasonable words across the street from where Sweet had purchased his home, and in the presence of seven hundred people. Did anybody say a thing? Did anybody rise up in that audience and say: "We respect and shall obey the law; we shall not turn ourselves into a mob to destroy black men and to batter down their homes, in spite of what they did on Tireman Avenue."

Gentlemen, these black men shot. Whether any bullets from their guns hit Breiner, I do not care. I will not discuss it. It is passing strange that the bullet that went through him, went directly through, not as if it was shot from some higher place. It was not the bullet that came from Henry Sweet's rifle; that is plain. It might have come from the house; I do not know, gentlemen, and I do not care. There are bigger issues in this case than that. The right to defend your home, the right to defend your person, is as sacred a right as any human being could fight for, and as sacred a cause as any jury could sustain.

That issue not only involves the defendants in this case, but it involves every man who wants to live, every man who wants freedom to work and to breathe; it is an issue worth fighting for, and worth dying for, it is an issue worth the attention of this jury, who have a chance that is given to few juries to pass upon a real case that will mean something in the history of a race.

These men were taken to the police station. Gentlemen, there was never a time that these black men's rights were protected in the least; never once. They had no rights—they are black. They were to be driven out of their home, under the law's protection. When they defended their home, they were arrested and charged with murder. They were taken to a police station, manacled. And they asked for a lawyer. And, every man, if he has any brains at all, asks for a lawyer when he is in the hands of the police. If he does not want to have a web woven around him, to entangle or ensnare him, he will ask for a lawyer. And, the lawyer's first aid to the injured always is, "Keep your mouth shut." It is not a case of whether you are guilty or not guilty. That makes no difference. "Keep your mouth shut." The police grabbed them, as is their habit. They got the County Attorney to ask questions.

What did they do? They did what everybody does, helpless, alone, and unadvised. They did not know, even, that anybody was killed. At least there is no evidence that they knew. But, they knew that they had been arrested for defending their own rights to live; and they were there in the hands of their enemies; and they told the best story they could think of at the time,—just as ninety-nine men out of a hundred always do. Whether they are guilty or not guilty makes no difference. But lawyers, and even policemen, should have protected their rights.

Some things that these defendants said were not true, as is always the case. The prosecutor read a statement from this boy, which is conflicting. In two places he says that he shot "over them." In another he said that he shot "at them." He probably said it in each place but the reporter probably got one of them wrong. But Henry makes it perfectly explicit, and when you go to your jury room and read it all, you will find that he does. In another place he said he shot to defend his brother's home and family. He says that in two or three places. You can also find he said that he shot so that they would run away, and leave them to eat their dinner. They are both there. These conflicting statements you will find in all cases of this sort. You always find them, where men have been sweated, without help, without a lawyer, groping around blindly, in the hands of the enemy, without the aid of anybody to protect their rights. Gentlemen, from the first to the last, there has not been a substantial right of these defendants that was not violated.

We come now and lay this man's case in the hands of a jury of our peers,— the first defense and the last defense is the protection of home and life as provided by our law. We are willing to leave it here. I feel, as I look at you, that we will be treated fairly and decently, even understandingly and kindly. You know what this case is. You know why it is. You know that if white men had been fighting their way against colored men, nobody would ever have dreamed of a prosecution. And you know that, from the beginning of this case to the end, up to the time you write your verdict, the prosecution is based on race prejudice and nothing else.

Gentlemen, I feel deeply on this subject; I cannot help it. Let us take a little glance at the history of the Negro race. It only needs a minute. It seems to me that the story would melt hearts of stone. I was born in America. I could have left it if I had wanted to go away.

Some other men, reading about this land of freedom that we brag about on the 4th of July, came voluntarily to America. These men, the defendants, are here because they could not help it. Their ancestors were captured in the jungles and on the plains of Africa, captured as you capture wild beasts, torn from their homes and their kindred; loaded into slave ships, packed like sardines in a box, half of them dying on the ocean passage; some jumping into the sea in their frenzy, when they had a chance to choose death in place of slavery. They were captured and brought here. They could not help it. They were bought and sold as slaves, to work without pay, because they were black.

They were subjected to all of this for generations, until finally they were given their liberty, so far as the law goes,—and that is only a little way, because, after all, every human being's life in this world is inevitably mixed with every other life and, no matter what laws we pass, no matter what precautions we take, unless the people we meet are kindly and decent and human and liberty-loving, then there is no liberty. Freedom comes from human beings, rather than from laws and institutions.

Now, that is their history. These people are the children of slavery. If the race that we belong to owes anything to any human being, or to any power in this Universe, they owe it to these black men. Above all other men, they owe an obligation and a duty to these black men which can never be repaid. I never see one of them, that I do not feel I ought to pay part of the debt of my race,—and if you gentlemen feel as you should feel in this case, your emotions will be like mine.

Gentlemen, you were called into this case by chance. It took us a week to find you, a week of culling out prejudice and hatred. Probably we did not cull it all out at that; but we took the best and the fairest that we could find. It is up to you.

Your verdict means something in this case: It means something, more than the fate of this boy. It is not often that a case is submitted to twelve men where the decision may mean a milestone in the progress of the human race. But this case does. And, I hope and I trust that you have a feeling of responsibility that will make you take it and do your duty as citizens of a great nation, and, as members of the human family, which is better still.

Let me say just a parting word for Henry Sweet, who has well nigh been forgotten. I am serious, but it seems almost like a reflection upon this jury to talk as if I doubted your verdict. What has this boy done? This one boy now that I am culling out from all of the rest, and whose fate is in your hands,—can you tell me what he has done? Can I believe myself? Am I standing in a Court of Justice, where twelve men on their oaths are asked to take away the liberty of a boy twenty-one years of age, who has done nothing more than what Henry Sweet has done?

Gentlemen, you may think he shot too quick; you may think he erred in judgment; you may think that Doctor Sweet should not have gone there, prepared to defend his home. But, what of this case of Henry Sweet? What has he done? I want to put it up to you, each one of you, individually. Doctor Sweet was his elder brother. He had helped Henry through school. He loved him. He had taken him into his home. Henry had lived with him and his wife; he had fondled his baby. The doctor had promised Henry money to go through school. Henry was getting his education, to take his place in the world, gentlemen—and this is a hard job. With his brother's help, he had worked himself through college up to the last year. The doctor had bought a home. He feared danger. He moved in with his wife and he asked this boy to go with him. And this boy went to help defend his brother, and his brother's wife and his child and his home.

Do you think more of him or less of him for that? I never saw twelve men in my life—and I have looked at a good many faces of a good many juries,—I never saw twelve men in my life, that, if you could get them to understand a human case, were not true and right.

Should this boy have gone along and helped his brother? Or, should he have stayed away? What would you have done? And yet, gentlemen, here is a boy, and the President of his College came all the way here from Ohio to tell you what he thinks of him. His teachers have come here, from Ohio, to tell you what they think of him. The Methodist Bishop has come here to tell you what he thinks of him.

So, gentlemen, I am justified in saying that this boy is as kindly, as well disposed, as decent a man as any one of you twelve. Do you think he ought to be taken out of his school and sent to the penitentiary? All right, gentlemen, if you think so, do it. It is your job, not mine. If you think so, do it. But if you do, gentlemen, if you should ever look into the face of your own boy, or your own brother, or look into your own heart, you will regret it in sack cloth and ashes. You know, if he committed any offense, it was being loyal and true to his brother whom he loved. I know where you will send him, and it will not be to the penitentiary.

Now, gentlemen, just one more word, and I am through with this case. I do not live in Detroit. But I have no feeling against this city. In fact, I shall always have the kindest remembrance of it, especially if this case results as I think and feel that it will. I am the last one to come here to stir up race hatred, or any other hatred. I do not believe in the law of hate. I may not be true to my ideals always, but I believe in the law of love, and I believe you can do nothing with hatred. I would like to see a time when man loves his fellow man, and forgets his color or his creed. We will never be civilized until that time comes.

I know the Negro race has a long road to go. I believe the life of the Negro race has been a life of tragedy, of injustice, of oppression. The law has made him equal, but man has not. And, after all, the last analysis is, what has man done?—and not what has the law done? I know there is a long road ahead of him, before he can take the place which I believe he should take. I know that before him there is suffering, sorrow, tribulation and death among the blacks, and perhaps the whites. I am sorry. I would do what I could to avert it. I would advise patience; I would advise toleration; I would advise understanding; I would advise all of those things which are necessary for men who live together.

Gentlemen, what do you think is your duty in this case? I have watched, day after day, these black, tense faces that have crowded this court. These black faces that now are looking to you twelve whites, feeling that the hopes and fears of a race are in your keeping.

This case is about to end, gentlemen. To them, it is life. Not one of their color sits on this jury. Their fate is in the hands of twelve whites. Their eyes are fixed on you, their hearts go out to you, and their hopes hang on your verdict.

This is all. I ask you, on behalf of this defendant, on behalf of these helpless ones who turn to you, and more than that,—on behalf of this great state, and this great city which must face this problem, and face it fairly,—I ask you, in the name of progress and of the human race, to return a verdict of not guilty in this case!

IN THE CRIMINAL COURT FOR KNOX COUNTY, DIVISION I
AT KNOXVILLE, TENNESSEE

STATE OF TENNESSEE	)	
	)	
VS.	)	CASE NO.
	)	
JOHNNY JOE CRASS, JR.	)	

This case came on to be heard for trial and was heard on the 9th day of December, 1994, before the Honorable Richard R. Baumgartner, Judge, holding the

Criminal Court for Knox County, Division I, at Knoxville, Tennessee, when the following closing arguments of defense counsel was had:

MR. TRANT: May it please the Court, ladies and gentlemen, on behalf of Johnny Crass and his family, I want to thank you for taking this job on. I want to thank you for your careful consideration, and I want you to keep that up. Now, I want you to carefully consider what you have heard and carefully consider what you would do as a reasonable person if you were in Johnny Joe Crass' shoes that night.

Certainly, what happened is a tragedy. There is no question about that. You saw Johnny Joe Crass say to the family of Brian Gregory how much he regrets his death. He wishes that it didn't happen, but it did. And it is time to end the tragedy. It is time to end the tragedy for Johnny Crass' family as well.

When you go back in the jury room, I want you to do me a favor, if you would. I want you to take just a few seconds, and everybody close their eyes and imagine themselves in that position that night, because hindsight is 20–20, and it is easy to stand here and say now what somebody should or shouldn't have done. But, when you are in those situations where you are reacting and doing split-second things, the test is: Might you have reacted the same way? Following that test, I think the answer would be, yes, I might have reacted the same way.

Certainly, the State has not proven to me beyond a reasonable doubt—

MR. BRIGHT: Objection, Your Honor.
MR. TRANT: For what?
MR. BRIGHT: Personal opinion, Your Honor. Counsel may not express personal opinions on the proof.
MR. TRANT: The State has not proven to you beyond a reasonable doubt? That is the law.
MR. BRIGHT: To me.
THE COURT: All right. All right. Mr–
MR. BRIGHT: That is improper.
MR. TRANT: I said to you.
THE COURT: I understand what he is saying. Go ahead.
MR. TRANT: The State has not proven to you beyond a reasonable doubt that Johnny Crass is an evil, wicked-hearted man, and that is what they have to do for you to convict him of second-degree murder, because they have to prove to you that he acted maliciously that night. That is just not the case. That is not the case. You have heard him testify, and that is not the testimony of a malicious, wicked-hearted man.

Let's look at the testimony, and I submit to you that the only credible testimony by people that were there and saw what happened came from this side of the courtroom, not from over here. You have got these people, Kelly Hatmaker and Tony Frye, who has testified repeatedly, repeatedly about inconsistent matters and not about little details.

I mean, everybody is going to get little details wrong from time to time. Anything you ever participate in, any of us, we are going to perceive it in different ways from time to time. But remember the way we talked about earlier, when you start to spin a lie, you forget what you said, what the lie says, and it is hard sometimes for you to remember how you have lied. So you tell different lies. That is what we have got.

We have got Tony Frye saying in the statement to the police, "Well, I went out, and I thought I might need my nightstick. So I got it out of the car, and then Brian grabs the bumper jack." Then, at the preliminary hearing, he says, "Well, I opened the trunk and got the bumper jack out." Then he says at the first trial, "Well, I came out and hollered at Brian, 'Here is the bumper jack.'" See how it gets more and more laid on as time goes on?

You know, sometimes when you lie, you mess up, and occasionally some of the proof actually comes out. Talking about the billy stick, "Well, I don't think I hit anybody with the billy stick," he says one time. Then he said, "Well, I may have hit somebody once." Then, another time, he says, "Well, I think I hit him several times."

Those were important things, because he is out there welding that billy stick as a weapon. Why in the world is he carrying a billy stick to begin with? For protection in case he gets into something, because he gets into fights? He and Brian Gregory are the kind of young men that go out drinking, and they are fighting drunks, and they get into fights, and that is just a fact.

I mean, you heard these last two witnesses we put on talk about Brian Gregory, and that is what he did. He was a fighting drunk. He would go out and get drunk, and he would get violent. You can't find people in church to testify about that. These people came from the penitentiary, and they are the kind of people, apparently, that Brian Gregory sometimes came into contact with, but they weren't connected up with Johnny Crass. They were connected up with Brian Gregory, and he was a fighting drunk.

That is a shame, because it cost him his life. If it hadn't cost him his life this night, it would have cost him his life some other night, and I submit to you that, if Johnny Crass hadn't resisted them, that Johnny Crass might be the one who is deceased here today. That is what self-defense is all about.

Think about it. Think about, if you were there, and think about what the testimony shows what really happened in that bar. What really happened is there was an argument over the pool game, and that two dollars, one dollar, and Johnny said, "Man, forget it," and Brian was getting pumped. And the more he got pumped, the more he wanted to fight.

There wasn't any knife in the bar, and you know that. Look at the people—look at Doris Henderson. Look at Jack Corum. They do not have any dog in this fight, and they were there, and they know there is no knife in the bar. Without that knife in the bar, Johnny Crass isn't the instigator of this. It was Tony Frye that picked up the bar stool. It was Tony Frye, and it was Brian Wayne Gregory who ran to that car and got deadly weapons out. And it was Lisa Whitaker who saw Johnny out in the parking lot with his hands up, dodging him.

Yes, the only thing he had to fight back with—and here it is—a knife similar to this. Ladies and gentlemen, if you are a murderer, and you are out to kill somebody, you don't carry a knife like this. What you would carry, if that were the kind of person you are is you would carry a bumper jack like this and use it against somebody, or you would carry a billy stick like this and use it against somebody, or you would carry a knife like this.

This, ladies and gentlemen, is a replica of the OJ Simpson knife.

MR. BRIGHT:	Your Honor, I object.
MR. TRANT:	It is one-half the size—
MR. BRIGHT:	That has no applicability in this case whatever.
MR. TRANT:	Your Honor, it is argument, and that is true.
THE COURT:	I agree. It is argument, Mr. Bright. Go ahead.
MR. TRANT:	One-half the size of the OJ Simpson knife. Otherwise, it is a replica. I know, because I know the man that imports them into this country. That is the kind of knife, if you want to go out, and you want to be able to kill somebody, that you are going to take with you. It is not a little pocketknife you use in scraping off your battery cables or using vinyl siding. This isn't a malicious person that carries this pocketknife. It is not a malicious person who is the peacemaker that night.

Do you remember Lisa Whitaker, and Lisa Whitaker did the best job, I would think, to try to explain to you what happened, and she said Johnny was a peacemaker. Remember it was Billy Shannon she was with, not Johnny. Johnny was the peacemaker, and he tried to keep these people away from him.

But think about it. Think about what you are going to feel like when a young, strong man is swinging this at you. I mean, it is going to scare you. It is going to scare any of us. Think about when another young, strong man is swinging this at you at the same time, and whether it is a bumper jack—whether he had the bumper jack at the time Brian Gregory was stabbed or not, I submit to you, isn't important. It is the state of mind that a reasonable person in that situation would be.

What is he seeing? He is seeing young men threatening him, calling him all kinds of names, picking up bar stools, taking this out of the car, swinging it at him, taking this out of the car, swinging it at him. Think about how he felt. What kind of fear would that put you in?

And he heard something happen with Billy, and he thought Billy was hurt, and he went to his rescue. What did he do? He got Brian up off Billy. He separated them. He put him on the car hood, and he held the knife up to him, and he says, "Get the hell out of here."

If he wanted to kill Brian Gregory, he could have killed him right then and there. But that is not what he wanted to do. He was the peacemaker, just like Lisa told you. He wanted to stop this fight, get these kids out of here, who had had at least eight, nine, 10, 12 beers.

Remember Brian Wayne Gregory's blood alcohol was a .26, and remember Dr. Jones saying that is very intoxicated. You remember Larry Bowman, who has known the family forever, saying that, when the kid got drunk, he fought. That is who you are dealing with that night.

If the bumper jack had been dropped—or does Johnny necessarily know that? Think what is happening to him right at that split second. When you get back to the jury room, please think about this and think about, if you were in that situation, how you might react. The way he reacted was this: Behind him was Tony Frye hitting him with this thing.

Now, this is a deadly weapon. There is no doubt about it. This can do a lot of damage to anybody. Remember Tony and Brian are acting together. Remember that. They are acting together. They are swinging these things together.

What is Johnny Crass supposed to do? This guy is hitting him from the rear, and Brian Gregory lunges at him to tackle him. Whether or not he has the bumper jack in his hand—and he doesn't know that—this time he knows he has had it, and it is all happening fast, but is he supposed to let him tackle him and let Tony Frye get down on the ground and beat him to death? Is that what he is supposed to do?

No, he has a right to defend himself against these two people who are attacking him at that moment, and all he has to do it with is this knife, and he reaches up, and he stabbed him. Unfortunately, it happens to hit his heart, not out of design. He didn't try to cut his throat or something like that you are going to do if you are really trying to kill somebody.

He reacted. He reacted out of his own fear for his safety, because he was being attacked from the rear, turns around to try to fight off that attack, and Brian Wayne Gregory lunges at him. If he hadn't reacted, I submit to you they would have had him on the ground, and they would have been beating him, bludgeoning him with this stick. That is what self-defense is. Each of us in this country has the right, if somebody is attacking us with deadly force, to save our lives or to save the life of a friend who we think is in danger.

The Judge will tell you, even if that fear happens to be mistaken, if we know now possibly that Billy wasn't really in danger, but you have a reasonable fear at that time, even if we learn later it was mistaken, that still qualifies as defense of another or self-defense, because it is what is in your mind at the time. It is what is in your mind at the time.

That is why you have to look so carefully and try to put yourself in that situation, because it happened so fast, and you react. He didn't have time to run. These kids are out swinging stuff at him. He doesn't have time to get away. What are you going to do, turn your back to them? We saw what happens when you do that. They come at you from the rear. That is exactly what Tony Frye was doing when the stabbing occurred.

To convict Johnny Joe Crass, you have to believe beyond a reasonable doubt the testimony of Tony Frye and Kelly Hatmaker. I submit to you that I hope we never get to the position in this country that we send people to the penitentiary based on that kind of testimony, especially when you have heard the testimony of people who are credible on the other side. We did not have to put on any proof. We are not required to do that. The burden is on them. It stays on them all the time, and Johnny Joe Crass is presumed to be innocent.

But we wanted you to hear the whole story, good and bad, as much as you could hear it. You know, maybe none of us should go to places like the Boardwalk Lounge, and I know Johnny Joe Crass isn't going to go to another place like the

Boardwalk Lounge. But he was there that night, and he was there with a couple of kids that like to drink, like to fight, and they like to use weapons, and they have done it before, and they will do it - Tony Frye will do it again, and Brian Gregory would have done it again.

They went after people with deadly weapons, swinging at them, attacking them, putting them in fear of their lives. Johnny Joe Crass was legitimately in fear of his life. I don't think there is any question about that, and he reacted, I think, as most of us would, if we were placed in that position.

Please, please carefully consider, when you go back there, what you heard from Johnny. You heard a man who is not wicked-hearted. You heard a man who regrets this and has lived with it every day since then. He feels for the family. No doubt about that. But you have heard a man, I submit to you, who made some mistakes. That night, he may not should have gone to that lounge, but he did, and he was attacked. He was attacked and put in tremendous fear, as any of us would be.

The bumper jack, the billy stick, it is serious, serious stuff, and you have the right, any of us have the right, the community has the right to defend ourselves against any kind of attack like that. If we ever take that away, then the young drunks who go out and start fights are going to run rampant, and we can't let that happen. We have got to be able to say, "If you attack us, we have got to be able to fight back to save ourselves." It is absolutely essential.

Thank you very much for all of your attention in this case. Thank you very much for listening carefully to the proof. Thank you for obeying your oath that you will hold the prosecution to their burden of proof, and that you presume Johnny Joe Crass innocent, and that we don't send people to the penitentiary for defending their lives or defending their lives for their friend.

The right thing to do in this case, ladies and gentlemen, is to come back and find Johnny not guilty, and I ask you, please, to do that. Thank you very much.

(END OF REQUESTED TRANSCRIPT OF THE EVIDENCE)

Epilogue

I have had the good fortune to see many of the places which meant so much to Darrow. I have traveled to Kinsman, Ohio and seen the octagonal house in which he grew up. I have traveled to Chicago and seen the Unity Building where he practiced law with lawyer and poet, Edgar Lee Masters. I have traveled to the famous courthouse in Dayton, Tennessee where he tried the Scopes case.

I have walked across the Darrow Memorial Bridge where his ashes were scattered in Chicago. Darrow has had a profound effect on my life and the lives of many other successful trial lawyers. His dedication to the law and to the underdog was unparalleled. The lessons he leaves trial lawyers will never fade.